TAKING
THE FIFTH
AND
RUNNING WITH IT

TAKING
THE FIFTH
AND
RUNNING WITH IT

A PSYCHOLOGICAL GUIDE FOR

THE HARD OF HEARING AND BLIND

JOSEPH D. REICH

BROADSTONE

Library of Congress Control Number 2015943530

ISBN 978-1-937968-18-2

DESIGN AND TYPESETTING BY JONATHAN GREENE

Cover photograph by Rhett L. Beck, used by permission.

Broadstone Books
An Imprint of Broadstone Media LLC
418 Ann Street
Frankfort, KY 40601-1929
BroadstoneBooks.com

He's like a mental patient who doesn't know
he's mental so he's perfectly content.

–Beautiful Girls

CONTENTS

Part Two   *Writing Love Letters to Those Lost Forever*

Part Four   *Stray Dogs, Winos, Tomboys & Whores*

PART ONE

COPING AND SURVIVAL SKILLS

The visit home,

The train used to drop us
off at that very desolate
spot right across from
Harlem-Valley Psychiatric
(where mother mocked
she gave birth to us)
with big brooding bars
of pick-up stick portholes
barbed-wire to keep in the juveniles
who were deemed and determined
to be a threat to themselves or others
as every so often you'd imagine
on some warm day in winter
how they might just air out
the electric-shock tables,
ping pong tables,
paperback novels,
paint-by-number
portraits & murals,
ships in a bottle,
cigarette stands,
hanging plants,
Adirondacks,
flyswatters,
firefly jars,
windy shutters,
the wild bird feeders,
even spooky silhouettes
spread out on drizzly benches
like drunken spiders dazed and
disheveled in the remote distance
(footprints and fingerprints

of coyotes and con-artists)
boxcar diners where
over-medicated
and sedated sons
would have explosions
on know-it-all fathers
(who apparently didn't
know a thing about them)
having treated them like
possessions now out of control
and dangerous, stealing anything
they could possibly get their hands
on as everything would instantly
turn uncomfortable and
awkward, deathly silent
(after all the defiance)
heavy heart would drop
yet it was kind of ironic
as whenever they picked
you up from *The Metro
North* at the last stop
from that eerie macabre
station with the surreal
name of "Wingdale"
to go out to their mansion
on the frozen lake in the mountains
things felt just as detached and distant,
desperate and despondent, dysfunctional
and indescribable; one might even
say foreign, unfamiliar, tense and
hostile after we had finished up
with all our small talk about
the ride up, and the sports
and weather, then like ghosts
would blank out, as we simply

did not have a thing to say to each
other, making our way through
slow-death, well-to-do towns
of The Berkshires where
no one was ever out there
and felt as silent and spare
as the last struggling breath
of some poor old man on his
deathbed, passing the pensive
and brooding ancient stone
clock tower looming
through the years
while felt like you
could hear the clear
muffled murmur
of its mysterious
internal organs,
rundown, roaring,
what customs eventually
do to you in the long-run,
its languid tick and tock,
wasted, wired, thinking
a coo-coo clock might
be more in tune, more
in touch, coo-cooing
on the hour; meticulously
manicured sprawling lawns
with no one ever around
higher than holy spas
high up on the hill
to hope to heal
psychological scars
of drama and trauma
of millionaire daughters
who had been wronged

by boyfriends who were
supposed to be father figures
there to somehow save them;
perfectly piled-up piles of wood
which went on forever (and even
in this area appeared competitive)
and clearly could only be cut
by the natives for these not
so gentlemanly gentlemen
farmers and may only be
acquired by workaholic Wall Streeters,
the wealthy New Yorkers and Bostonians,
old money who appear like ghosts and phantoms
never home, just there for appearances, to simply
make an impression with wives with no expression
and plenty of room(s) to make excuses, priceless
pieces of precious antiques put out on display
never moved an inch out of place to provide some
self-absorbed, distorted (non)sense of time and space
control freaks, curators, trying to keep it all perfectly
sane and in the effort to overcompensate, turn
even more mad and crazed, blessed barnhouses,
covered bridges covering snow-capped rivers,
libraries and factories draped at the base of bare
birch mountains with silent snow-white towns
stapled to the horizon and creeping thyme
citizens somehow missing in action
(your old passive-aggressive pals who
used to love to push buttons at formal
wine and cheesy get together wheeler
and dealer philanthropic fund raisers
and sarcastically pose the question–
"Prove that you exist" as the guests
instantly got defensive, turning void
and vacant, even parasitic and pissed
literal, ridiculous, clearly not getting it)

returning back to the meticulous museum
and mausoleum where they always had
purchased some brand new contraption
rare and exclusive one of a kind tchotchke
with dozens of dead ladybugs passed-out
on their backs on wraparound porches
in the pall of a sacred and solemn sun
beginning to melt snow in the perennial
garden like a bastard child landing butterfly
kisses on the alabaster cheek of his mama
petrified pines hovering high, as though
windswept branches got suspended
in action from a last blast of winter
the creaking floors and crackling fire
crows in branches like the top hats
of madmen, rippling rocking lake
house weighed down with weather-
worn oars and paddles whose aroma
smelled like the lost lily pad lichen
of lagoons passed down from generation
to generation, the regenerating rotten core
of civilization, as the hypnotic haunted echoes
of seaweed skeletons shimmered through shattered
mountains; a Shaker table whose fragile fissures got
bigger, expanding or contracting due to the change
of seasons and triggered and started to feel all those
old feelings begin to creep in again of a deep and
desperate sadness and anger, of which you could
never ever get control over, some muted howl,
eternal existential sigh where you just wanted
to break down and cry and started to find if
you tried you could take great comfort and
pleasure regressing a little to those bizarre
and peculiar images you had just recently visited
in your stopover at Harlem-Valley Psychiatric.

The life & times of the aqua-velva man,

Existence came to be
through some shaven pussy
of some sweet suburban snatch
in a deep green plush backyard
in the late-Sixties; a country built
& bent on assassinations & domino
theories & secret CIA intelligence
plots to murder & overthrow third
world presidents for purposes of self-interest
& imperialism through violence or propaganda
you name it whatever works best and whatever
gets the job done (The American Way) taking
out disagreeable uppity foreign leaders
who will only prove to make problems
for The American Way of Life for the
picture perfect innocent American
bystander for that girl you're
fighting for back home
(goddamn there are so
many slices & pieces of shrapnel
in The American Pie) real-life deals
by devils & corruption & ultimatums
& blackmail & billboards & quagmires
& shortages & recessions & that slow-
motion which we just naturally accepted
& remained etched in our social & cultural
consciousness of that ski jumper in *The Wide
World of Sports* hurtling down the mountain
suddenly wiping out & tumbling out of control
showing the fine line between 'the thrill of victory
& agony of defeat' like the old time milkman for
no particular reason awkwardly tripping over

his feet and the bottles just breaking into a
million pieces taking trains home drunk high
on rum & Coke from that cart on the platform
some savior & self-soothing instant-gratification
where you no longer knew the time nor season
no longer knew thyself just the train schedule
& departures & arrivals on the grand board
that magnificent scroll whose towns would
suddenly show up with anxious anticipatory
triggers and just get you back and deliver you
to a place which seemed like home somehow
somewhere lost some time down the road
sometime a little before & after rush hour
advertisements of successful Caucasians
and that one token non-threatening
black man having one hell
of a good time living the life
living the lie, a life of leisure
high on some very thick and
rich liqueur like *Bailey's Irish
Cream* all collectively giddy
from some deep shallow
sweeping secret inside
joke only they're privy
(which all in that
suspended stop-
action spontaneously
and simultaneously
cracks them up)
trying to make you
a part of but always
somehow feeling outside of
fading away in the florescence
from Grand Central to the misty
nightmare dream of the suburbs

the call-out at the station
which startles your senses
like mandated electric shock
therapy & separates fantasy
from reality, beauty from brutality
& reminds you time to get the hell
up & get out & your stop & gotta
wake up & some strange brisk
breeze suddenly smacks you
smack-dab on the cheek like
a farewell kiss from a girl
you been always dreaming of
& awakens your being but not
really not really quite exactly
sure so you start to stumble
& fly like a wounded sparrow
with an arrow through his soul
out the door into the transient
geometric silhouetted world
to a place & form you
once called home.

The importance of sunday morning tv
somewhere around the 1970's
(broken down on a clinical and didactic level),

Boy Billy Batson
otherwise known
as *Shazam*! with that
handsome bronzed
bone structure inn-
ocent indigenous
Native-American
accent sounding
like every natural
configuration
from the copper
hill clay canyon
who came into
our homes every
Sunday morning in
the bare burnt-out
radiant wilderness
of the baking desert
(there were also
those good ole
mobile homes
and bi-ways
involved)
and were told
how he came
to be or was
conveniently
reborn by like
some perfect

storm hovering
just above
in the form
of all those
old wise ancient
mythological gods
they named from
top to bottom
(just like
you were
forced to
memorize all
the presidents
and capitols)
and transformed
into his sky-blue
polyester made-
to-fit crime-
fighting uniform
from the conflux
of wind and spirits
and storms topped
off with lightning
and thunder and
all of the above
(some kids have
all the luck) and
suppose that old
ancient advice
and wisdom
and support
from those gods
we all wish we
got in real life
was actually
in real life

having
real-life
florid visual
hallucinations
just trying to
make it just
like any one
of us poor
lost souls
with our
fucked-
up families
(and scenarios)
and how they
so inaccurately
judged and
portrayed
us and what they
unfairly unjustly
expected from us
and how you inevitably
ironically were forced
to hit the road from
The East Coast out
of a subtle loss
(not subtle at all)
no one could possibly
even begin to know
somewhere between
underestimation
and harassment
and brainwash
and Billy Batson
became that lone
American Indian
ghost-phantom

as you found yourself lost
disoriented right there in
the middle of the desert
silently modestly nobly
pointing his finger over
the mountains to tell you
over there's The Pacific
while in your childhood
memories and consciousness
seemed like a whole other
existence where he lived
and existed somewhere
just outside *The Waffle
House* outside that exotic
foreign land they like
to refer to as California
somewhere in the wide
and expansive sands
you imagined was
a far cry from
the hop skip
and jump
suburbs
just outside
The Grand Canyon

How did that
song go again?

"dunt dunt dunt dunt dunt dunt
dunt dunt dunt dunt dunt dunt
dunt dunt dunt dunt dunt dunt

heart and soul…"

All those worthless life lessons,

I don't know never really understood when they told you
how team sports would teach you all these life lessons
and ethics and principles and how it would build and
shape and mold your character as to me taught me
everything I didn't want to know about character
and other people's character hanging out with
some of the biggest fake tough macho obnoxious
prepubescent alpha-male assholes you'd ever want
to know (or not want to know) trying to kill each other
and couldn't stand spending one single second with them
whether on the cross country track team (my buddy and
I always ending up sneaking off in a mad dash stealing
cupcakes from the local supermarket and eating them
by the train tracks when the whooshing rush hour trains
would come rumbling back from Manhattan) playing lacrosse
being so freezing cold watching my palms turn a purple-blue
and arms and legs in so much pain forced to have to hold it
all in (not sure what lesson they was teaching) feeling tears
rolling down my cheeks and wondering when we were gonna
ever get home and when it would all be over when it would
end and the world would end and now about thirty years
later driving home through a very similar environment
very similar like dusks through the hush of wishy-washy
repetitive scenarios of ticky-tacky aluminum siding
split-levels and ranch style homes wondering
when in the hell is it all really gonna begin?

Cheeseburger, fries, & coca-cola from the red rooster to harlem valley pyschiatric to the berkshires,

I think I'm really starting to relate in my middle ages
to when we were children and used to read such things
like *The Guinness Book of World Records* and remember
like all the blissful monotony and madness of repetition
and in retrospect such a fine line between willpower
and discipline and obsessive-compulsive behavior
but also had a self-soothing like quality about it
as touched on the eternal loneliness of existence
and the solitary madness and persistence of such
freaks (of nature) like there used to be this guy who
was so big they said they had to bury him face down
in the strings of his piano for his casket, Tom Thumb
or was it his cousin Thumbelina perched in the palm
of some gigantic Caucasian in his gray flannel tall-
man at the circus suit, I think some dude who had
such quick reflexes able to catch bullets in between
his teeth and things which amazed me or what amazed
me not in a particularly pleasing way about the fickle
and fucked-up nature of man like that list of the most
hated people of all time and somehow Richard Milhous
Nixon always beating out Hitler each and every year
(while one just had really poor judgment and appeared
reactive and impulsive and the other far more plotting
and proactive in his willingness to take out a whole culture
of people as though human nature was far more forgiving
of a megalomaniac and strangely hyper-critical of a rigid
overbearing and controlling manic maniac) so decided
to turn the glossy pages to far more benign things like
Tiny Archibald from Beantown, Pistol Pete Maravich

from The Big Easy and Rick Barry from Golden State
with that underhand free throw and like the greatest
shooting percentage of all time and Wilt the Stilt scoring
100 in a game and averaging 50 for a season and other
such queer and random facts and statistics but somehow
as a kid it all feeling so relevant like the amount
of consecutive hours dribbling basketball for days
on end and paddling ping pong balls till the end of
time as similarly find my days this life goes down like
the stray soothing sound of helicopters on the dying horizon.

The fonz flying over those barrels in milwaukee, wi

We had some
fleshed-out
stick figure
tippy-toe
cross the tippy-top
of The Twin Towers
of The World Trade Center
couple decades ago & remember
that smudged newsprint picture
in the paper on our breakfast table
way back there in the nineteen-seventies
like it was just yesterday high up there
in the smog & pollution of my hometown
of New York City as a holy wide-eyed
mischievous kid with mad soul & spirit
(N.Y. Times to be more exact– "All
The News That's Fit To Print") with this
idiot madman #2 son trapeze artist thought
holy shit that's complete craziness someone
who just appeared to have way too much time
on his hands & had the nerve & balls to do it.
Couple decades later had fanatics fly planes
into it & strangely enough having become
so damaged over the ages was able to
actually believe it & really not able to
comprehend it until like some long-lost
profound psychological trigger about ten
years later suddenly hit me intuitively out
of nowhere having been there & a native
New Yorker ironically weeping in a newspaper
truck while delivering papers at dawn in some
god awful godforsaken suburb; just recently

had this daredevil dude (think they said was
the seventh generation of one of those Flying
Wallendas) tightrope the drip-drop sandcastle
geological formations of The Grand Canyon
right over that beautiful expanse of the Colorado
River & remember I think somewhere around
the mid-seventies that madman Evel Knievel
in red white & blue bicentennial uniform
flying over it on his motorcycle, not sure
if he made it or not (was actually irrelevant
as everything when it comes down to it really is)
like the fearless Fonz flying over all those barrels of
gas? Beer? Also queerly inconsequential in the fictional
suburbs of Milwaukee, Wisconsin & stopped him
freeze-frame suspended in mid-air until we had
to wait the impulsive, little creatures we were
for the next episode literally like a week later
same bat time same bat channel. We've had
several people out of desperation probably
for pretty damn good reason take their lives
jumping off The Brooklyn Bridge & Golden
Gate Bridge & had the first quote on quote
American finally traverse the pockmarked
face of the moon after a ragged & wasted
clothesline string of assassinations & then
make some grand fantastic humble histrionic
confession somewhere way up there out there
in the competitive constellations. These days
we appear to have a whole population of kids
& singles & idiot housewives & landscapers
looking all self-important addicted dedicated
delusional & codependent on their cellphones
& contraptions so I don't know in my opinion
we still just have not quite managed to capture
or find that little slice of Heaven secret magical

potion & solution to ever get happy or contented
kind of like ever finding the cure for the common
cold if you kind of somehow get what I'm talking

Would have loved to have met that guy who
got inspired to write that blues song *Blue Moon*…

The invisible plane,

Wonder Woman we hear
                    stammering
                              slurring her words

    over *The Home-Shopping Network*
                              having spent

    her night taking shots
                        at one of those
                                  chain restaurants
                                              on the strip mall
with Leroy from
"Fame" fame

                  asking if they may
          have any remaining
of those ricochet

                    bracelets or truth lassos
            to make things right again
      from all those relationships
gone bad

                  left her feeling empty & hollow
      & deserted & abandoned

            (no man…

                  on the border
                        of Borderline
                              & Munchausen)
          abuse a real-life

(lowlife) vicious
& repetitive cycle

    leaving you running
            round & round in circles
               with more questions than answers

desperately searching for patterns
          but deep down inside (not wanting
             to admit it) just the fucked-up

          shit of human nature…
     constantly taking it

out on yourself
      asking what did I do
        to deserve this?

          eternally stranded

              with heart broken
           & soul shattered

       (futile & forsaken)

           that invisible plane
             still running
               with

kickstand
    down
       outside her split-level
     suburban home
  spitting jet fuel
     like some souvenir

conch shell
             at the end of the world

All the kids next door
            floating on top the pool
                        from drug overdoses

        while no one in the neighborhood notices
obsessed with their perennials.

She wonders
(thus her
derivation)

3 easy payments
5-7 business days
sounds perfect

Can make this
her recovery
period.

For charlie,

I think I've lived a pretty decent well-rounded life
and gotten a taste of it all; recall doing painting
and contracting for this real nice and tough
guy who used to be a paratrooper during
the war which was one of those do or die
jobs no joke which took mad courage and
one of those true-blue down-to-earth boozers
you could trust and rely on and had a heart of
gold and when I finally moved neighborhoods
and was looking all around for a job anywhere
I could find one he called back to give a character
recommendation for *The Pink Pussy Cat Boutique.*
Man I really miss that old timer and all the cases
of beer we used to down and reflect on and one
liners and punchlines we used to crack after
having put in a good and long and hard day
on the job and from the last I heard of him
he finally packed it all in and moved down
to that land they call Florida which to a certain
extent always saw as extenuating circumstances
had the desire to save up his whole life just to retire.

Je ne sais pas hope he found a part
where they don't harass you and
leave you the fuck alone as to me
that there is the real sign of freedom
what it means to live happily ever after.

A whole other part of michigan they don't speak of,

I miss that rich girl from Michigan I used to spend summers
with in Manhattan when we were getting our masters at
Wurzweiler School of Social Work who had such a great sense
of humor and dry wit and was so eccentric and damaged
and frigid would speak hard core porn and knew all the actors
and actresses but when it came time to get affectionate would
freeze-up and almost act offended when she had told all
our mutual friends she always had a crush on me but
someone who was great to spend all my free time with
up there in her air-conditioned doorman condominium
in the stars in The Upper East Side and one summer day
suddenly said let's act English and call each other cunt and
it was cunt that and cunt this and tell you it actually felt quite
cathartic without all that obvious and predictable American
political correctness doing this with a very rich girl from
Michigan who was codependent and worshiped her father
the physician and probably why she could never ever really
give of herself affectionately or physically or erotically or
spiritually why she probably never proverbially or literally
cut the cord but someone who I really miss and someone
who I had a hell of a lot of fun time spending time with (even
though she was impossible and impulsive and so erratic with
her moods and behavior) and with similar sensibilities
and aesthetics and people and groups of people we
loved and hated and it was cunt that and cunt this.

Shortest distance not always necessarily a strait…

I think the only flag
I ever been loyal to
are those medieval
tapestries hanging
from the walls
of Cloisters
in uptown NYC
which seemed
to divide the
wilderness
and that
part of
the city
winding
down to
the punched
out lights of
misty buildings
whose
towering
sycamores
& heather
gardens
like some
postmodern
Pearly Gates
& Garden of
Eden during
overcast opaque
leaf blowing days
chestnuts knishes
stirring insane

looking into the deep
faded stitching
of mythological
beast/beauties
for some sense
of purpose
& meaning
even belief
or maybe
just once
those people
places & things
who wouldn't betray
during school days
of separation-anxiety
heading back home
when the sun
broke over
The Palisades
brooding reflecting
along The Hudson
cars stripped down
to the bare bone
by the now you
see 'em now you
don't scavengers
along The Bronx
River Parkway
with those
proud brave
noble long-lost
explorers from
foreign shores
posing with blustery
ripped sails heading

bumpadabumpa 'neath
The George Washington
to try and make names–
"Hey, can anyone
tell me where's
Sleepy Hollow?"

A didactic study of the human soul,

I want to know the trigger to the trigger
to the trigger of the trigger to know
ironically and perversely deep down
inside is all really the personification
of what it truly means to feel hollow
Chopsticks, *heart & soul you left me*
however that goes then you know
it's just smooth sailing maybe
a stop off at Newport Creamery
back paddling down The Hudson
to where all the explorers showed
& saw The Palisades on their left
& Cloisters on their right heading
upstate passing young Teddy
Roosevelt's boyhood estate
& study of specimens
& butterflies up to
The Borscht Belt
The Adirondacks where
they kept all the famous
half-crazed Yiddish slapstick
comedians & prisons & institutions
getting pretty decent reception off
their transistors in the summer
dreaming of their freedom &
a return back to Spanish Harlem
& The Diamond District & Vaudeville
Lower East Side Third Avenue A B & C
Delancey & Katz's & Ratners & Gus' Pickles
hobbling bleary-eyed, disoriented, drunken
over The Brooklyn Bridge back to South
Brooklyn Casket where all the young

luscious senoritas wave from their
blood-red curtains just off Caskiosko
Degraw St. Carrol Gardens while only
the midnight winds & wild
shadows can swirl a certain
waltz leading you somehow
back up the stoop to the
vault of the vestibule to the
ragmop foyer up that long
merchant marine banister
which has seen so many
drunken dramatic dances
dragged through the keyhole
& drop dead at last fast asleep
on your mattress in the marrow
of your nightmares where all your
dreams in disguise live happily ever
after connected to the clothesline
which never had a fighting chance
somewhere between guilt & expectation.

How to head home through the diners,

In this life
in this existence
in this institution
called marriage
there's such
a fine line
between
being a bum
& madman
between
being
a goon
& god
& do
the only
true-blue
long gone
options become
having to escape
to the mountains
to the taverns
to the disco
just past
the steeples
& trailer parks
driven mad
driving
in the driving
rain insane
not giving
a damn (doing
talk therapy

to yourself)
sans wind
shield wipers
in your long
lengthy wild
flowing falling
snow white beard
& simply sitting
there with some
somber psychotic
smile sentimentally
plastered to your face
observing all the girls
while getting a good
buzz on at the bar?
I remember when
I used to haunt them
& see them literally
getting hand jobs
right on the sly
like old slick thieves
& young daughters
from the block
in the deep dark.
I've seen them
literally sitting
all day long
in the park
no matter the season
no matter the weather
winter spring summer
fall especially the fall
when the night
just began
to fall

turning
wise & old
nowhere to go
& knowing it all
& before
you knew
it like stray
cats & dogs
they were gone.

The stars,

I'd like
a review
of a motel
just after
some
hus-
band
gets
grew
some
alley
murd-
hurt
literally
screwed
for-
eign
extra
mar-
doll
awe-
fair
won-
der
if
can
get
any
good
chi-
nese
a-

round
there
views
from
the
slum
from
the
suburbs
from
the
crumbs
of the
post-
card
car-
ou-
sell
wisp-
purr
to
your
loved
one
in the
back
of
cop
car
as
they
all
gather
around
like a

funeral
pro-
session
at the
sweet
& sour
chicken
when the
crickets
start
snick-
ring
it's all
in the
twin-
call
of an
eye in
the iris
& fall
& life
& times
of what
they do
to you
to try
& break
you
great
place to
start a family.

Why even try?

How to convince the wife when you tell her
you want to take her to Vegas and she says
we're not going to Vegas! And you tell her
we're going to Vegas! And she says I don't
want to go to Vegas! And you tell her we're
gonna go to Vegas! (Christ on a cracker!)
Use the argument like when Ben Affleck
and his wife got into a fight and flew off
to Vegas and have we gotten to that point
in our life and marriage when you surprise
her on the spur of the moment and have
to beg and convince her and give her
demands and ultimatums and she
says all this nonsense about renovating
the bathroom or putting down floors
or getting granite or buying her that
diamond which got ripped-off and feel
like you're playing this constant existential
game of catch-up not sure why and wasn't
the whole point to simply do something
out of the ordinary and on the sly in
taking her to sin city and never leave
our rooms for the whole weekend like
when Howard Hughes stricken with
the Hamlet dilemma was all paranoid
in the prime of his down slide as you
hear your child like some wild angel
sloshing in his bathtub in the back
ground having the time of his life.

Non-existence (and proof of the metaphysical world)

Interviews are always
like Descartes' old proof
of "I think therefore I am"
where they always want you
to prove how much you
can prove and you're
always thinking in
the back of your
head how much
you just don't
want to be
there.

Your home away,

Walked into the bathroom of *Walmart*
today and the toilet read "Toto"
and knew finally at last
I was home...

This fine red-haired girl
who was very diligently
putting those discount
dvd's into that great
big watering hole

where madmen
and dope addicts
and every lost soul

displaced from
the neighborhood
nod out told me
if I needed help
with anything
to just ask her.

I thanked her
and she had no idea
nor for that matter in
truth and reality did I.

Bullets & bacitracin,

Is it just me or am I the only one convinced
that the queen has really poor taste in hats
and power suits but they continue to keep
on hysterically waving at her in her chariot?

This summer I'm gonna plan one of those
vacations for me and my wife and kid
down to The Magical Kingdom and
drive down from the mountains
of Vermont to Orlando.

Most likely I'll seclude myself in the hotel
and may have one of those social phobias
better bet just hate tourists yet do believe
I owe them as much and is that
so much to really ask for?

In marriage you try to make the best of it
looking out from your private silent terrace
over the palm trees to that long stretch
of narrow bridge vanishing out to
the horizon of Rimbaud's Florida

content just to know
they're happy hopped-up
hopping around the turrets

somewhere around
Cinderella's castle.

You wonder if they got
any good take-out
out there…

Bloom (a window just outside sleepy hollow),

Foghorn tells you everything
       you always wanted to know about nothing

                (the essence of mortality...)
lone sailor blowing shofar till eternity.

What is that strange sensation within anonymity
       where you get to know so much better
              the self and being?

 (Weird movies advertised at the depot
       you are convinced you know
          and no need to go
            based on this keen rapport)

Weather is everything which streams up your nose
            when you are alone.

    It all shrugs, it all moans–
     mmmmmmmh! mmmmmmmmh!

Voyeur,

The history of the world
long groan of a foghorn
gotta do all the leg work
just to get some swatch
sent to you from Utah
why we turn to drugs
to stray dogs
to psalms
long Bunnyhop line
at the bar-mitzvah
blues "This Is It"
by Kenny Loggins
Michael McDonald
"Sketches of Spain"
by Mr. Miles
insomnia by William F...
Shakespeare & Eugene O'Neill
the daffodils don't come up
year after year all you care
about The Cactus League
in Manifest Destiny
Spring Training
no one making a name
as all you hear over TV
is hot peanuts! cold beer!
oranges and orangutans
put that gorilla to sleep
from those *Samsonite*
luggage commercials
gave the death penalty
to elephant who stomped
those tourists for throwing

cigarette butts at him
Marlon Brando played
by Stanley Kowalski?
stalking himself through second-hand
shop looking for films of himself
mountains have begun melting
and condors back once more
sailing in sky-blue heavens
crows have personalities
as well like a lone Chaplin
waddling in top hat & tails
(new clues and shrapnel
from missing planes
over The Indian Ocean
dinosaur bones found where
the Mormons chose to settle)
no need for punch lines and riddles
for nightmares, redemption, and theme music
the only time they get back to you is at your funeral
that Asian crooner in sequins on that ferry to Sicilia
rising up out of the sea on the distant misty horizon
no need for analogies or adages about Atlantis
(see where Kate Middleton went topless
what happened to Brigit Bardot and Jackie O?)
leftovers from your mistress in midnight refrigerator
still waiting on that swatch from The Rocky Mountains
balmiest to date and still cannot show up to the factory.

On The Lay Of The Land (a list poem)

One may compare Darwin's survival of the fittest
adaptation of species to the change of topography
and demographics and population when they put
the state courthouse up out here and the convicts
decided to settle down; to follow like Noah's Arc
or a traveling carnival with its tarp ripped off…

Chris Columbus	gi joe (kung-fu grip)
Henry Hudson	mr. quarterback
Magellan	raggedy-ann
Lewis & Clark	stretch armstrong
Desoto	loop de loupe racetrack
Champlain	barbie (and all her phases)

Family tree of criminals & thieves
                    shedding leaves…

Domicile,

1,   torn left at the heather

2,   go down the road a mile
    or so little less little more

3,   pass the endless heavenly
    field of deep decadent corn

4,   pass the cathedral
    of crucified souls

5,   pass the tourists

6,   always pass the tourists
    & never look anywhere
    in their general direction
    as will always put
    you in very specific
    conflict & confusion

7,   pass the very quaint
    & exclusive hoity-toity
    haughty, higher than
    holy bed & breakfasts

8,   take a deep breath
    again like holding it all in
    passing the mausoleums
    & gargoyles & seraphim

9,   pass the alpacas
    & donkeys braying
    who have lost their will
    to express themselves
    & have turned to distant
    muffled train horns that
    will save your soul

10,   pass the jesus christ
    lizards who walk on water
    who walk on rivers leaping

from lily pad to lily pad
11,   pass the foghorns
       & take pictures
       right in front of them
12,   pass the depot that
       the schitzophrenics
       live in the back of
       & smoke cigarettes
       & make inaudible sounds
       always the exact same hour
       & can set your watch
       & the train schedule
13,   pass the weeping boys
       letting it all out & keeping
       it all in in the group home
       which nobody knows
14,   wipe your cold sweat
       gooseflesh dope addict
       flesh-colored skin
       in the wasteland
       of wilted flowers
       & step right in
15,   do not disturb that pretty
       pouting girl who eternally stands
       silhouetted, brooding, just as you
       thought, planted in the weather-worn
       window of oceans of corn, pondering
       the problems of the world, figuring it
       all out & not telling a single soul
16,   do not touch (or harm)
       a living breathing soul
       as it's all very fragile
       persecuted & wired

17,   shut your eyes & imagine
       & fathom geometric
18,   shapes & figures
       pass your dreams & keep going
19,   & go over the industrial river
20,   spit blood into the rain bucket
       & realize finally at last
21,   you are not there
       & have reached
       your destination.

A geographical map of folklore,

I want to assign symbols to the wind rain and snow
to the rivers and mountains and rocks and minerals
to the seasons and transition of seasons and beautiful
sentimental triggers and moods that they put you in
that they all bring on all that brooding all that lost love
all the lustful fantasies you hope to bring on once more
nothing obvious like a weather map or Egyptian scroll
yet something simple and geometric when I'm feeling
at an all time low and feel like everyone is gone and gone
for good for no particular reason I know nor care to know.

I want to assign symbols to dreams and nightmares…

Creeping thyme,

Have you ever had one of those days
where you tried to see if you could
make some dream last the remaining
part of the day where for whatever
reason you could think of (and tried
your best not to) it just seemed so
necessary not to let it slip away
where you tried to make that
feeling last for an eternity
as it was so much more
appealing than anything
that could possibly be
offered by superficial
society becoming your
core reality and wished
and hoped and prayed
that this spiritual and holy
feeling would never go away
this seductive secrecy which
was so much more convincing
than any role or ritual or tradition
or belief this passionate beast which
engulfed any guilt or grief built up
in your *super-psyche* this hope and
dream which penetrated every
pour of your being that just
seemed to hold so much
more truth and meaning
than anything in your
(over)bearing and
(im)possible
waking...

Getting through the daze,

Recently been having this vision
of the whole Peanuts gang nodding
out on heroin, heads really hanging
perhaps around that poor crestfallen
Christmas tree where all the pine
needles have posthumously fallen
with the fizzling lights, droopy star
teetering on top, all messed-up around
the mound by that makeshift lemonade
psychiatrist stand, or that wall where Linus
and good ole Chuck Brown make their final
stand, bow their heads, grief-stricken, contemplative
and question, Socratic method, kind and compassionate
their existence, contented, watching days pass right
in front of them, and see both their perspectives, their
moods and behavior, then crash with elbows eternally
leaned-up, head in hand and earnestly, existentially
discuss dreams and goals, resolve conflicts and try
to figure out the futile, impossible problems of the
world, the pained and perplexing suffering soul
exchanging thoughts and ideas and future plans
right where the seasons change, but scene always
seems to remain the same, the trees and leaves
and tops of bleak twinkling roofs, steeples,
temples, mosques, mausoleums, streets
and lamplight sputtering with a pastel
sun falling, big bulge of breathtaking
moon rising, turning from day to evening
leaving simply those stray starlit stoops
with a whole wistful windswept village
swept up in blessed silhouetted geometric
forms and images of the sobering season.

The hyperactive and psychotic and driven
Snoopy who I never much cared for
his overconfident personality
Marcy and Peppermint Patty
finally finding each other
Pigpen misunderstood
underestimated
Franklin the black
kid never taken in
Lucy the loud mouth
who just never shuts
the fuck up, but who
knows maybe I'm just
going through some sort
of mid-life crisis of sorts
most likely not and am just
trying to find ways to cope
and catch up on everything
I believe I missed out on
from a very complex
and competitive
overbearing
and overwhelming
passive-aggressive
impossible Jewish culture
does that make sense at all?
And so thus maybe just prefer
seeing the whole Peanuts gang
strung-out on dope, not saying
a whole hell of a lot
a bunch of distant
disobedient dwarf
dope addicts
completely
out of it

contented
centered
blissfully
nodding out
to that brilliant
bee-bopping piano
and brush drums
of a mean and
moody magical
Vince Guaraldi solo
building up then fading
off in the background
all of them naturally
shuffling home
on their own
by their own
choice and
volition
pace and
space and
time and
leisure in
a constant
state of flux
through the fading
glow and opaque
drizzly autumnal
leaf piles of some
divine dwindling
disappearing season.

On the profound nature of maxwell smart,

I think God has been having one hell of a time
at my expense lately, but what ya gonna do?
He's God and well I'm nobody and all beyond
my control all my appliances have been breaking
down my heart breaking and been a shell of a hell
of a lot happier if we were all those straight-faced
saintly comedians from that hit sitcom *Get Smart*
those slapstick secret agents like 99 talking into
our sneakers having top-secret conversations
in the cone of silence surrounded by the ones
we love with those great spreads of cold cuts
like at some bar-mitzvah some mafia get-together
but what am I who am I to say "would you believe?"

Time-life,

They should sell the elixir morphine
in a variety of multi-colored liquids
midnight-blue forget-me-not truth
glistening in those twilight sunset
midnight pharmacy windows
for medicinal and nostalgic
and pure pawnshop purposes
like lovely leftover liqueurs
your parents used to display
in those geometrically
shaped bottles they
got as gifts from
their schmaltzy
practically insane
friends in the suburbs
really with drinking problems
but back then not a big deal
just to make life bearable
somewhere in the very
early Sixties never
seeming to really
be touched out-of-touch
like antiques taking on
a tinctured dusty nostalgic
mythology gracing the shelves
of mirrored bars your dad the dentist
built which he never quite finished
but still looked brilliant and being
the perfectionist he was pointing
out the parts he didn't get to from
his *Time-Life* book collection reminiscent
of days of morphine addicts when people

could still be taboo and tentatively still in
the closet in the basement where you could
build great swinger bars from the *Time-Life*
book collection to set up scenarios and situations
which never ever really quite seemed to happen.

The affects of weather on human behavior,

Picture the image of sadomasochistic wife & husband
walking around the *Super Stop & Shop* on a fine Sunday
morning with the snow falling down in the parking lot
and whipping out the whip and giving him a subtle shot
"Slave I need an avocado! A mango! That sweet & sour!
Chock full-o-nuts! Buns! No! Not that one slave! That one!"
After they have completely stuffed the car with groceries for
the week they go into the library as he sneaks a peek at the
pretty young high school girls with bubble butts; librarian
who's the perfect perfectionist ordering all the young high
school boys around. When the dynamic duo wife & husband
team get home he asks permission if he might be able to
spoon and snuggle with her milf girlfriends but promises
he won't get turned on. Drools a dream on his son's pillow.
When she ignores him he asks if he might be able to go back
to the *Super Stop & Shop* as claims they forgot to pick up
the frozen yams he's gonna make for their *La Choy* chicken later
on. She tells him that it will be good and feels closer to him
'cause he's far-sided and she's near-sided and drops a punch
line something along the lines of leading each other around
in their old age bumping into things and these types of things.

Snow starts to pile like moon pies outside the window...

What husbands do late saturday night,

After having sex with my wife
I tell her I'm gonna slip out
to work on my delusions.

She asks me if I'll need
a Phillips screwdriver.

The distinct difference between the thief & criminal,

I have always felt totally comfortable around the thief
(as found him to be hard working, salt of the earth
and the efforts he would make to climb the ladder
or more accurately fire escape of success) while
in many ways knew that was the best that he
could do and where he was from and in many
ways appeared to really have no choice in
the matter, whereas with (the efforts of)
the Caucasian criminal in the upper-middle
class echelon and strata always consistently
felt alienated and the eternal stranger and
a certain sense of self-loathing and that I did
not belong something they consistently always
tried so hard to make one feel but eventually
with the patterns of existence and survival
able to view them with a certain sense
of the absurd and buffoonish in all
the things that they try to do to
convince others and play roles
and keep up appearances almost
little something like The Marx Brothers
or The Three Stooges at The Grand Ball.

Small talk: how they treat you down here,

I don't know…they're always famous…that Eyewitness News
Team for being the first on the scene…your #1…exclusive…
voted for 7…reporting some sort of Jesus…or Virgin Mary
sighting…some sort of miracle…some sort of unidentified
savior…some image or vision or smudge…lingering up
there in the dressing table heavens and depressing and
dismal dirty dusk of winter…in the middle of one of
those miserable moonless nights…*just one of the one million
stories…in the naked city*…and this be one…some time just
after supper…between bumpadabumpa…and the weather
…and yes I guess…like everything else don't expect them
to save me…not even asking…but how about at least once
that glow or smudge coming down…just once getting down…
just once for the hell of it…for the time being…from way up
above the Morningside Heights corridor…from the radiator
from the landlord who refuses to give me heat…from the
dozen frozen chilly trees in the evening park…from the
rooftop…from The Bronx House of Detention…from
The Industrial Home for the Blind…from Lower East
Side…Sansimium slapstick Pitt St. fire escape…from
Chinatown…from Brooklyn Bridge…from the puffing
factory on the river…from midnight…from the dawn
…from the stray dogs…to the stars…just drop by for
a nice cup of java & pleasant small talk…a little nosh
…I'll meet you on Avenue B & 12th…where Lucky
Luciano got his start…no one's gotta be the wiser
…and promise I won't betray you…or stand you up…
trust me…I've been there millions of times before…back &
forth…forth & back…learned the ancient art of empathy
& compassion…or even for that matter…to be human…

whatever the heck that is…a modicum of politeness…as
down here…I swear…it just gets so damn lonely & phony
& obvious & repetitive…& will transfer from that misty
drizzle vision in the window to someone who truly gets it
& is sympathetic & promise won't take you for granted…

PART TWO

____

WRITING LOVE LETTERS

TO THOSE LOST

FOREVER

Odessa's,

How long before completely catatonic
before you just lose it from all the unholy
phony-baloney liar hypocrites of existence?
When you lose your whole support system
or never really ever had one to begin with
& finally at last vanish into the matchstick
fable & folklore spirit of condensation?
Well I'm gonna tell you; I'm gonna first
get myself one of those combination platters
& plunk myself down at *Odessa's Diner* on
Avenue B & 7th downing blintzes & kielbasa
& stuffed cabbage, while the hustler dope
addict adolescent delinquent keeps on ducking
in & out, splitting, ditching, running in out on
his old man to cop his fix to try & fix all those
feelings of feeling inadequate, consistently lied
to & cheated & manipulated & betrayed & taken
advantage & trying to make sense of all those
mixed-message mangled-mind-dead mixed-up
bullshit & old timer resigned to learning to have
to accept it & looks like his face has been stretched
from Hell to Heaven like some old pale-gray slow-
death blank newsprint tenement which has finally
caught up with him & can no longer pawn or pass
the buck to some secret inadequate art of rationalization
or Freudian recommendation favor owed to him, wheel
& deal blackmail bribe ultimatum of psychotropic
medication, while all that's left is son's skeleton &
raw nerves & paroxysms of built-up & buried explosions,
carefully planned quips & contradictions, instant grati/fic-
titions & confessions & condemnations, consistent broken
promises, addictions, desertions & abandonments, those exits

& entrances! Exits & entrances! Exits & entrances! Existence
a series of ghostly exits & entrances! Cigarette & coffee
wishes, broken record histrionics, broken mechanical,
sad machinations, the broken tooth women & pretty young
Ukrainian waitresses, old eccentric dramatic homosexuals
with their seductive, sarcastic, corncob comic strip smiles,
sitting solitary style at their tables, talking up a storm, eyes
spinning around counter-clockwise going through the
routines & rituals of demonstratively pointing at menus
& probing about side dishes & specials, then settling for
their traditional Greek salad & afternoon cocktail, while
skittering autumnal leaves come tumbling into windswept
doors & secretly settle into the folklore of heavily trampled
floors in cracks & crags & corners below the old woolen
coats huddled on hooks & hangers at last finding yourself
settled in mad karma Nirvana familiar in the distance and
distant with the familiar, more comfortable within the
anonymity of strangers than the parasitic gossip & rumors
of backstabbing, cookie-cutter, two-faced neighbors holding
onto grudges, soulless, bloodless whose expressions look like
they want to just take hostages & make you just as miserable
those great spacious bathrooms where no one can
ever reach you, get you, find you & finally stop
& take a deep breath & (re)collect your thoughts
& regrets & dignity & self-respect; Batman in his
bat cave with needle & razor & bullets & bible & fear
of intimacy & at risk-behavior, while Wonder Woman
breaks down once again in her discotheque uniform,
rearranging her mask & mascara & roles & becoming
reborn & you return to the trapdoor of your soul taking
your place in front of steamy seasonal windows, seeing
all your past fleeting dramas & trauma, all madmen
& runaways & phantoms & scholars
old Black Panthers & Hell's Angels
shadow puppets & stick figures

engaged in secret missions
fragmented yet industrious
silhouetted in a whisper
beneath the falling
curtain sputtering
streetlamps of the season
dog people & people who used
to be rich hoteliers & men whose
women all walked out on them
wheeling & dealing in the park
& old farts in their plaid checkered
hats & mothball overcoats looking
like they just got off the boat &
pigeons as much a part of this
as any of these restless ghosts
lost & lonesome desperately
searching self-destructive
souls looking to cope
& put an end to this all
Gyro without the sauce
Mashed potatoes & peas–
"Gimme a straight highball whiskey!"
& Jimmy the speed dealer simply
stealing away in his half-crazed
smack-dab profile of self-denial
with his fate & karma like some
estranged superhero contented
having come to terms never
to be seen from or heard from
again disappearing bidding
farewell on his flaming
thin-skinned silhouetted
now ya see 'em now
ya don't skateboard
all the way out to

the haunted & holy
stapled stained-glass
horizon by some burnt-out skeleton
stadium on the mystical East River
where retired florescent fishermen
& The Banana Pudding Man make
their final stand at The Hothouse
beneath The Brooklyn Bridge
as you simply sit there
right there in your
diner window
with a view
of the street
with a view
of the universe
in the bare blessed
pitiful beautiful
dysfunction
of existence
no longer with any
bullshit or resistance
explanations or excuses
conflicts or resolutions
as you discover as
always it's always
in abeyance
in the silence
of the moment
in the senses
in the flux
of transience
in reflection
feeling the sun rise
& fall & rise once again
without virtue or sin

completely at one
comfortable in
the glowing
slums of
imagination
washing it
all down
with seltzer
& a slice
of lemon.

**That fine little slice of new york island
no one knows about not too far off
from grand central and the river,**

When I bring
down my blinds
where I feel so much
a stranger it allows
me to finally think
back to my days
in Manhattan
when I used to
work swingshift
at the front desk
of that hotel
owned by that mean
man who hired all those
nice and kind Indian brothers
I used to love to work with
and joking around made me
feel part of the family hearing
in the not too far off distance
the pitter-patter of pouting horses
hoofbeats of mounted police
mixed in and mingling with
the pumps of all those sad
solemn secretaries eagerly
and reflectively returning
back to their buildings
with their heads
held up high

in that perfect little
twinkle of twilight
the doorman with
a drinking problem
nodding out and
every so often
looking up
and looking out
like some lost beacon
with a hopeful smile
for something better
for his homeland
for some brand
new sort of
girlfriend.

Grocery list: to live & die & get by,

1, Crucify me & nail me
to the wide pine floors
2, The pumpkin pine
3, Stolen pies in sill
4, Painkill me plainclothes junkie stealing up fire escape
5, Soon to become son found dead in alley, insane brother
humiliated hollering at sister beneath rainy Sunday matinee
6, Trying to make a name! Trying to make a name! Just trying!
7, Beautiful bully tomboys starting up in schoolyard
charming vampire bankers from the subway at dusk
8, The leftover aroma of roasted chestnuts
& hot pretzels from the houndstooth
Hell's Kitchen section of Manhattan
9, Paint me by numbers that only you are capable
only in russet & crabapple & forest-green & violet
10, Whip me & me be both protagonist & hero
of your silent stag ragtime film like one of those
used & abused old time slapstick vaudevillians
11, Only scent at the concessioners being rubber
cement & oranges & formaldehyde & pork-
fried rice & blintzes & stuffed cabbage
12, Up & coming coming-uppers literally
being chased down 2nd Avenue waving
unpaid checks by hollering maître d' & waiters
13. Rich kids getting a kick out of it nodding out on heroin
14, Light a cigar, light a candle & clamp it to my skull
like one of those long poles you bolt & slant down
from doorknob to floor to keep out the criminals
whose breath smells of diesel & pig knuckles
in the gaslit cobblestone of Orchard & Ludlow

15, With a view of the backyard & cows who
have escaped once more along with crawling
delinquent super heroes over the stone wall
16, I shall make my way through the seasons
& chimneys & crosses & shore, tap dancing
till eternity, till hell freezes over, slide,
shuffle, slide & hopefully, miraculously
17, Melancholy, be scene no more
18, Hoboes making s'mores
19, Weather be wind screaming
20, Shutters slamming in storm
21, Monkey bread & prayers
caught between the law & The Lord
22, Long lost rainy days exploring labyrinth
catacombs of second hand holy & haunted
subterranean Magazine St. stores madmen
& fallen Confederate southern gentlemen
antique wives' pristine precious treasures
23, That antique woman who was always there
for you & had been left abandoned at the altar
now perverse, perverted, romantic & explosive
24, Long lost contemplations along The Mississippi River
only thing you learned, only thing college was good for
25, The madwomen like ghosts, ghosts like folklore
26, Peddling your bicycle home, excruciatingly alone
when the lonely night settled in, now clearly knowing
you know no one at all, forgotten by the world, when
the moon starts to glow, seeing it all through the keyhole
of the peephole of mausoleums murdered & resurrected
by the constant vicious deep dense thick po'boy
aroma of sweet magnolia, wafting, penetrating
your nostrils, your being, your bones, your soul

27, Everything turning to spirits, so surreal & slow
only knowing this after feeling like you've lost it all
& seen it all & learn & love & sincerely know it all
28, Surviving off cornflakes & bananas & staticy Ol'
Satchmo barely hanging on, striking a match to light
the gas to the fire of the grill to the radiator, like an
eternal beacon which kept your heart beating, the
eternal prisoner, the damaged son survivor to guilt
& anger & conflict & triangulation of not being
able to live up to the wishes & expectations of
a martyr of a savior who just merely saw you
as an extension, knowing you'll never ever really
return home cause they'll never ever really know
(nor care to know) understand what you been
through & will never ever possibly have a clue
29, Later on The Hothouse along The East River
with a midnight view of Brooklyn in Winter
meeting black girls from Yonkers leaving the
cemetery nunnery to become alcoholic nurses
30, Me in the solitary confinement hospitality business
with old madmen who used to be in the merchant marines
named such things like "Pee-Wee," slurring concierge
muttering to himself, who would literally like clockwork
go mad every time just around midnight on the outskirts
of The Bowery on the outskirts of sanity between steam
Chinatown & Little Italy with such down-to-earth titles
31, Like *St. Marks* like *The Pioneer Hotel*
32, Lock me down within a porthole so's
I can look inwards, outward & in once more
33, I'll raise a plastic goblet backwards filled
with sangria to the floor to all the whores I've
known who literally turned my life around

34, Stone me with your betrayals & I shall recycle & bicycle
with a great big smile & have a blissful picnic with child-
like fiancée & lovely wild black families along the shores
of Cloisters on The Palisades of The Hudson in the prison
of your jism of your phosphorescent, polluted metropolis
35, Aimless bridesmaids & angelic ballerinas
turned to hookers & scholars & wanderers
36, Nameless naked black girls turned to statistics,
incarcerated by Lower East Side pigs, disgusted,
not in the job description
37, Fold me up in your shadows & bullet-ridden
soul & I shall crawl back into my nightmares
& find out what it was all for
38, Gravediggers on strike
39, Time for tea & animal crackers
40, Sun streaming through like tuna fish & matzah.

A mandolin in the pharmacy window,

My wife picking up dice for my four year old kid who
loves dice the look and feel of it at the monkey in a barrel
apothecary tuxedo made out of seagull how you used to stroll
heavy heart ship wrecked soul around the reservoir in New
York with your psychiatrist who back then seemed like
the only one who gave a damn your only friend sometimes
feel it's not so much depression but all the circumstances
and situations that lead up to it and if we could just get
rid of all that fucked-up shit all that mixed-up essence of
resistance we'd be free home free never quite knew what
it was like to be free except maybe taking the train home
drunk in the late early evening to my lonely light cradled
radiated at the end of the boardwalk at the end of the world
in Coney Island mesmerized hypnotized entranced transfixed
still under the influence watching all wild beautiful black girls
like some rare pearl bopping ballet giggling hysterically going
back and forth telling and exchanging real imaginative stories
the queenyard the trainyard gazing out the window of your
grandma's looking out at all the brokedown bum boxcars
of Jamaica Queens spending the rest of her days chatting
on the bench with her longtime longlost friend a rose by any
other name be Rose Hershleifer and the old Puerto Rican
lady much younger taking care of her both mutually not
understanding a word the other was saying to each other
your grandfather the pharmacist out in Bedford Stuyvesant
Brokeland who spent every waking hour never taking a day
off selling (ice) cream soda sandwiches ointments and elixirs
even heroin over the counter one of the few Jews in an all
Sicilian neighborhood shuffling home exhausted dead tired
through the razorblade zip gun shadows with a bottle of
kosher wine babka and *Brooklyn Eagle* newspaper wandering
every so often after work literally strolling over The Brooklyn

Bridge to Manhattan to take night classes just to learn the
language his brother my Uncle Arnold his right hand man
who helped man the counter and his other brother Jack
who no one knew what the hell he did most likely a bookie
as he was frequently seen silently stuffed cowering comfort-
ably in Sunday corner during almost every family occasion
with that beautiful broken matzah brei face kind eyes and
yarmulke balanced on top of bald head a transistor to each
ear one following The Mets and the other following The
Yankees matter of fact as the so-called story seems to go
literally dropped dead when The Mets won the '69 World
Series you spending your summers slaving carrying golf
clubs for rich soulless stockbrokers spending your few
extra bucks going out with friends bronzed
handsome stuffed in station wagons to go
on Bronx Runs picking up Hawaiian Gold
from brothers on the corner contemplating
out your window dozing off dreaming of
the rich daughters and wealthy obnoxious newly
married girls big butts stuffed in plaid shorts from
the golf course from the day before in compromising
positions taken to whole other lands whole other existences
listening to Bob Marley The Clash Bob Dylan over barking
dog butterfly garden coming to the conclusion life is just
really one big simple difficult and dysfunctional game
of musical chairs truth or dare hopefully not some
big boring futile game of he said she said if you
ever really cared to get where I'm coming
from if you know where I'm coming from?

My relationship with a corned beef sandwich,

Thanks for the place. Came in most handy. We fed ducks
to the breadcrumbs and met a psychiatrist and his kid down
by the pond. Seemed to know some of the same people, yet
got it bit mixed-up with colleagues and patients and myself.
Had a kid in the second grade and D. of course in the first,
but was very shy so decided to just turn around and direct
and guide him and point my finger towards Tuckahoe, as
was involved with his son in some sort of action-adventure
looking for the train tracks and trying to find their way back
home. We walked back through the village to pick up a
couple scoops and told Dylan we had to go through the
tunnel under the train tracks. He asked how is it possible
to go under trains and loved how he framed it that way.
When we got there we shared some ice cream together
and was some of the best ice cream I ever had and solemnly
listened to Bruce Springsteen's "Santa Claus is Coming to
Town" while seeing all these single lonely wealthy women
who seemed to have no one, wandering through the pale
silent town. I heard the geese take off to the navy-blue
clouds of darkening dusk turning into quiet night with
their rapturous honking and the comforting distant muffled
honk of trains and rhythmic rumbling like the sudden wash
of some synchronized wild breeze through plantation
shutters, heading back and forth to do their rounds out
to Grand Central. Erica was visiting her mom in The Bronx
and said she ran into her crazy friend's Ma on 231st who was
blabbing out loud in the middle of it all, all about some brand
new drama and how she always had some new scam and
hustle with her husband and a bit disgusted how this was
how they always seemed to survive and get by and now
were suing some doctor who Erica very profoundly a bit
Joycean appropriately Malapropian not even knowing it

referred to as "the suers" and this time claimed the doctor
had messed up his arm but the feeling was starting to come
back and with their profits were gonna go to California and
Hawaii. When Dylan and I got back from our journey he
tumbled up and down the big steep hill with those fallen
leaves from the sugar maple (sorry the leaves always seem
to fall bigger and better in New York suburbs and can only
really know that unless you grow up there and stays with
you forever within your colorful childhood transcendent
consciousness and imagination) and there was this shadow
of an old man pasted up against his opaque window watching
him wasted like a butterfly pinned to his collection. Later on
in the night when I waited for Erica for her taxi from The
Bronx I just saw him sitting all solitary all tragic all by his
lonesome in his big empty rectangular whitewashed room
beneath a single solitary watercolor painting and a black cat
kept me company beneath the streetlight and felt like my
only friend in the world and thought I could definitely die
happily ever after a distinguished old man solitary soul just
being left the hell alone bending over the terrace taking in
the crazy rain gazing at the glazed green emerald phosphor-
escent decayed skyline like some suicide sighing drip-drop
cathedral sandcastle. I thought about planting tulip bulbs
and them coming up the next season reminding me of the
configuration of that song "We shall overcome...We shall
overcome." From the distant windowsill I watched the sil-
houettes of people who appeared to be pleasantly shuffling
with purpose and meaning in the faraway twinkling lights.
We survived off halvah and clementines. By mistake left
frozen fishsticks and a couple black & whites in the freezer
and sorry can't seem to find the clicker. Later on Erica
brought back from The Riverdale Diner a corned beef
sandwich and dived right into it and devoured it
in one gigantic gulp.

The antique's roadshow:
a study on human behavior,

Usually when I climb up on my treadmill at night I like
to turn on something exciting like *Antique's Roadshow* but
recently the way I been feeling around the holidays and hit
with a mild case of the melancholia couldn't care less about
other people's corny family histories or their sweet and
innocent and sentimental memories and being something
of a trained therapist will instantly and naturally be able
to gauge and access their affect and expressions and body
language and how genuine and if they get a good estimation
see how they suddenly seem to really love that relative and
get all reflective but interesting how quick that emotion turns
to a motive and become self-interested and those memories
don't really seem to mean or matter so much and got that
look like where and when can I cash in and everything-must-
go with that simple and see-through glow or if they are
disappointed or devastated or disrespected and brought
back down to their baseline of functioning only triggering
that much more being let down and cursed by this cruel and
brutal fucked-up existence switched to never really ever liked
them or cared much for them anyway in the first place dirty
and filthy rotten disgrace and by both reactions interestingly
ironically with that selfsame great solemn pall of silence
before and after they provide the assessment either don't
seem to really care so much anymore about those warm
and heartfelt sentimental memories but more so can you
tell me if you got a check cashing place around here or fuck
it am gonna just get a couple cases of beer and think you
more so would prefer some dude who was far more genuine
perhaps wasn't so goddamn predictable and phony-baloney

maybe even with a bit of the minor case of Tourette's
Disorder with features of paranoia spouting out paroxysms
like you're so full of shit motherfucker! You're a freaken
rip-off artist! Swindler! A pillow biter! Rat bastard! I should
knock out your fronts! Staple your nuts together! Be so much
more a breath of fresh air and not holding it all in pretending
to be all charming and shit and so much more real and down-
to-earth and instinctive and them having to do a physical
restraint on him while as a distraction the wobbly TV camera
will pan in and do a close-up of the beautiful bronzed statue
fountain of that turn-of-the-century seductive siren smiling
and simultaneously hearing in the background I'm gonna
kill you! I'm gonna kill you if it's the last thing I do!
Kind of the way I been feeling a little bit recently
around this joyous time of gift giving.

Stanzas of a deadbeat dad,

Erica was cutting my hair with a scissor
      and it triggered when she was a little girl
      her father used to leave his beard in the sink
      and she said it was the only time she wasn't
      sad or angry 'cuz it meant he was still there
Later on when he left, her and her mother were
      just left there both eating tv dinners at two
      separate trays in two separate chairs watching
      television (this became something of a custom
      and tradition) 'cuz she said it made the pain
      hurt less, as if in this casual state of transience
      it just made it easier to accept, more like guests,
      like ghosts in partial denial, not having to be
      part of the lifestyle which was suddenly forced
      on them somewhere up there in some big dark
      flashing living room on the 12th floor in the bronx
      right around that park right around the reservoir
He was a banker and the cheapest man you'd
      ever want to know and used to make them
      bring orange juice to *mcdonald's* as they would
      bicker all the way out to pennsylvania dutch country
Much later on when he tried something of a
      reunification and showed up with his wife
      the last woman he had cheated with, first
      time he met me tried to manipulate me
      to persuade erica to resent her less and even
      asked her to put back on her wedding dress
      and traipse through the kitchen so he could
      try to imagine and recreate and recapture
      some vision he once again had missed
      and was just not there for

Sometimes it makes me so sad and sympathetic
   whenever i think about all the shit she's
   had to go through and endure…

A criminal's christmas…
(with stressors and anxiety included),

Turns out after they finally transferred her grandfather
who was a postman and became a two million dollar-
aire to *The Hebrew Home* in The Bronx her Uncle Butch
came back to pick up shit from his past but not exactly
the sentimental stuff you would expect like pictures
or books or records or yearbooks but all the guns
and rifles he had secretly stashed without her
grandfather even knowing it in his bedroom.
Guess those couple years upstate in *Sing-Sing*
didn't do much towards rehabilitation or make
much of a difference and can take the man out
of the but can't take the…or whatever the hell
that expression is? Took all the funds that was
supposed to go to her mother and manipulated
the grandfather and had diamond rings and
such items that was in her safe deposit box
transferred over; sort of ironic as Erica's
father, the banker, who cheated on her
mom with multiple women, while the husbands
showing up to their door saying they were gonna
kill him and used to be haunted by messages left
over their answering machine played over and
over again of "Staying Alive" during the disco era
then after picking up all the loot Uncle Butch headed
right out with his new lovely bride for a long weekend
to Vegas and then back to his daughter's in Chicago.
This is just a fine little example of our extended
family and support system, classic, instead
of picking up the sentimental shit went
back to pick up his guns and rifles
to imagine have one last final blast.

Somewhere between darren & dagwood,

Sometimes just sometimes with all the slow
death dumb routine & ritual of domestic life
he says this just can't be just can't be paradise
just doesn't seem right (is this what they mean
by *the institution* of marriage?) when he walked
the plank when he walked the aisle when that pastor
spoke those famous last words speak now or forever
hold your peace why didn't one of those fucked-up
freak friends of his or acquaintances with those silly
sarcastic smiles stuck to their mug once stand up
and at least give it a shot once give a shout-out
(he knows he sure as hell would have) and take
over the role of preacher and now understands
upon reflection all the mad drunken dancing
and dapper and distinguished and solemn
jazz band respectfully going through
the motions but it was a damn fine
ceremony it really freaken was
and just the scent of those
fragrant red blaze leaves
of autumn was as precious
as any of those moments
in childhood and just that
in itself made it all worth it
like some surreal real-life
game somewhere between
truth or dare & fantasy
& superstition.

On the nature of cravings (or feening) after years and years of thank you for your patience,

1.

All of the world and modern civilization began
from the deep dark empty hollow hole of the fish's
jaw who after a couple billion years decided to sprout
claws and in that one moment instinctively cognitively
crawl onto shore for reasons still unknown (Survival?
Adaptation? Simply bored and needing to hit the road?)
and explore somewhere between the corals and jungle

2.

All of history in my opinion began and ended on tattoo beach
in Coney Island where all those needles and prophylactics
and carnations washed up to the mad shores chock-full
of The Brothers and Guidos from Bensonhurst and
Sheepshead and some enterprising Puerto Rican
with his shirt off and sunglasses on like some
dazed and damaged half-crazed barker
strolling disoriented in sync in between
the hypnotic rhythms of the crashing
ocean hollering soulful spiels and mantras
like– "Fudgie! Fudgie! Bud-wiz-a! Fudgie! Fudgie!
Bud-wiz-a!" and you decide to go with the latter
and suck it down and try to hold onto your buzz
as long as you can in the moment and forget
it all under the insane beating Brooklyn sun

3.

He lifts a conch shell to his ear in utter awe
mouth agape just like that fish from so long
ago and like some ancient tape recorder hears
the history of the world— "Mo! Mo! Mo!
How do you like it? How do you like it?"

PART THREE

SCENES FROM

THE CLINIC

Magritte,

Suddenly from
a distant blue void
somewhere between
yesterday and tomorrow
a bleak streak of light
creeps up to office
window almost
seeming to
welcome
and usher
in the secret
shift of seasons
like an empty creek
of shadows calm and
contemplative when
there is that stray
and fragrant
yet subtle
aroma
which will
become some
pensive leaf pile
of which you spent
more than a little while
hiding and escaping, contemplating
a confused childhood and even more
foreboding future where you might
happen to let your imagination run
wild and pictured this is what it must
feel like to be in Heaven, penetrating,
plunging, floating between mysterious
and magical (piled up and down the street

like solemn safe sanctuaries, like perfectly
packed pagodas and pyramids by sturdy
and stocky Sicilian gardeners, almost welcoming
your anatomy for own private solstice of autumn)
Sometimes it seemed as these leaves cut a crease
right through the blazing wilderness through
pure hollow emptiness awaking forgotten
spirits winding and stretching an existence
far more promising and intimate
when suddenly you are transfixed
by a stir of leaves that spontaneously
show up out of nowhere and for that
one brief moment dare to feel settled
and self-aware, strangely satisfied
with the ephemeral transient
state of all
that's inside
and everything
that's out there
and are glad to know
that you are finally alone
and feel so much more at home
and imagine this is what it must be
like at the inner crossroads of the soul
kind of like some Magritte mural where
the interchange of light mingles between
day and night without you really quite
knowing or really caring to know why
you feel so spiritually and subliminally
turned on by some bleak streak of light
bending brightly through a cloud like
the iridescent tragic hush of a Caravaggio
paintbrush, Van Gogh's visions and Mister
Magritte's sudden pang of pleasure feeling
so perfectly in touch with some out-of-touch
far-fetched, and long-lost, far-gone treasure.

Taking breaks,

1.

Suspiciously you sneak out antique shops
into the magnificent splendor of autumn.
There is a frothing river and school boys
who still stop dead in their tracks to try
and capture the hypnotic wail of boxcars
as if this liberating blast may somehow
once more remind them of who they are.

2.

Baby-fat girls with gold medals draped to gym uniforms.
You breathe out the lost and lonely folklore of linoleum

3.

Forgotten fishermen who have been
secretly wound-up shuffle across the cobblestone.
Missing-in-action fathers creep from dead man alleys

4.

The judge is an alky and when we were wise ass kids
growing up drinking the punchline always seemed
to end in something like– "I'm sober as a judge
Sober like Judge Fagan that is!" and then
would collectively break out laughing

5.

Hung up child
who got hung out
to dry by a horrible
mother is now a hung up
old timer who hangs on for dear
life like some lost ornament hung
up on the same hocus-pocus corner

6.

Humming hand-me down hymns outside
St. Mary's Barber Shop right around rush hour
thinking that maybe this might keep it from raining.

He's got us all believing, while along come
the funeral men and crow who keeps a watch
out over the whole town; over the old Victorians
and graveyards; you wonder who was Saint Mary
and how come they never seem to leave last names?

7.

Directly across from the monuments and memorials
the fountains and benches of forgotten children who
have now taken on the roles of junkies and hookers
while the Christmas tree and biblical characters
spontaneously brought back to life and staked
up for the season with weathered signs which
interestingly read such things like "Dr. Payne"
"Dr. Kneedle" for dentists, or for attorneys
certain comical captions like "Ernest Tongue"

8.

When all the bagpipes
& pillars & steeples
all the pubs & people
doughboys & ghosts
& witches & widows
have been packed up
ready for the blasts &
bullet holes & all the
rough drafts of winter

9.

Statuesque state cops keep a close eye out
on the building which burnt down some time ago
and has become the vernacular for nosy neighbors
who play the perfect role of strangers and witnesses
yet when most needed have proven not to quite live
up to the courage of their conviction busy and brave
with their gossip and rumors (people like this have
always made you feel so frustrated and lonesome
and how much there's really no one there
for you or that you don't exist at all)

10.

The cosmetologists are graduating and hard-working
humble girls continue to make their rounds at the diner

11.

It all smells like minestrone.
Suicidal priests on the bridge
and sober sexless ladies from
the historical society who
have not gotten it in ages

12.

They have lost their personality
Good boys are still rumbling…

Self-portrait of a self-portrait,

Campaign slogans leer across lawns of haunted houses
on the dried-up river beds that ramble through town
on the hills drowned out in crosses and used-car lots

where keystone cops, corrupt clowns
seductive tomboys and madmen kids
hang out and try to find their way out.

This is a very strange place where little people
swipe at low-flying planes, horrific husbands
peddle stationary bicycles on driveways

stunned and drained
and devoid of expression
like the aftermath of an assassination.

Fake aristocratic women in Jackie O. sunglasses
smoke menthols like Dolce Vita actresses
huddled in front of mental health clinics

where the police men
and parochial school girls
come in for anger management

after school and before their shifts
with a view of the ghosts and phantoms
and boxcars delivering bananas and granite.

The old distinguished pornographic pharmacist
searches for lost girls by the ocean, while blushing
mothers push strollers rambling through burning cedar.

The days you cherish most without a doubt
was as a child, a thief ripping off candy bars
from merchants which really was your father

unaware of it, acting-out, sneaking down the tracks
to the river to meet fellow delinquents for your dose
of instant-gratification, denial, passive-aggressive heaven

then head headlong home with head hung low
at sundown, guilt-ridden, when the hustle was over,
crashing, and knowing you were really supposed to be

doing homework reaching your potential
(like some monkey-puppet ripping off strings
and costume after the drama reached its pinnacle)

hidden some-
where deep
between

obsessive
and
compulsive

"How
much you
benchin'?"

Third cousin removed from heimlich maneuver,

They met at the physical restraint class
for group homes and fell madly in love.
She was no dummy, he was, no matter,
pretty much interchangeable, and made
a connection on a physical, emotional
and spiritual, psychological level
both living real damaged fucked-up
lives and had the need to be held or
held onto or held tight. There's this
keen phenomena during such types
of dynamics and training exercises
where you know you can only let
go once they actually start crying.

On the nature of "the cog,"

I always loved that expression– 'I'm just a cog…'
as always seemed so damn apropos and descriptive
like declaring in a very proud and declarative defeated
manner I'm just a total fuck-up and incompetent, like
that other infamous statement 'I'm just doing my job'
and thus by the natural consequences and laws of
human nature am gonna make you suffer just like
myself, so I suppose if you cog/nitively-behav/iorally
just look at them all as a bunch of cogs may help to
self-soothe and calm and put it all in perspective?
I used to work as a social worker in one of those
fine and compassionate mental health clinics
in the Commonwealth of Massachusetts and
this girl, one of the nicest and kindest down-
to-earth souls you'd ever want to know, who
worked in medical records and was just
trying to do her job had to deal and cope
with this sleazy slob of a psychiatrist who
used to keep on asking her to reach down
to the bottom charts so he could stare straight
down her blouse; a children's psychiatrist,
mind you, and every time you walked
into the chart room she would suddenly
I swear just jump straight out her skin
having been traumatized right there on the spot
(ironic in that mental health chart room) by those
crude and vulgar come-ons and amazing even when
she complained to the head cog in medical records
in the mental health clinic who sounded like a robot
and happened to be a female just like herself, nothing

ever got done as if the mad scientists had taken over
and this sleazy children's psychiatrist, I guess might
over right (or the high-holy hierarchy of a bigger cog
over a little bit of a smaller cog over the smallest and
hardest working cog of them all) was able to keep
his job until she just eventually couldn't take it
anymore and picked up and hit the road, while
the next girl who happened to be an experienced
stripper (guess *survival of the fittest* or more
so meeting the job description) proved it
wasn't so easy and convenient for him
to take advantage and eventually he just
vanished into thin air, like I suppose all
the other sleazy bullshit and assholes
out there, and all those very fine, fair-
weathered citizens who like to play
the role and refer to themselves as
just poor lost souls in an unfair unjust
world or more so just cogs in a system
caught between the haves and have nots.

Quarterly review,

The other day I decided to just open up
the chart of one of the kids I was seeing
and read his psychological hx which went
something like– "presents as depressed
evidenced by having to fall asleep with
television on with so many clothes and
books piled up on top of his bed he will
not clean up and he sleeps on the floor"
and thought this kid is exactly like me
and I'm really going to be able to connect
with him but then I thought just a bit longer
and deeper about what was I really going
to be able to say to someone like him?

She draws her bad dreams for me,

Something like
a see-thru girl
hair burning.

You wait for this kid burnt-out in the hall
with your eyes closed like some junkie
on the corner in San Francisco hearing
the hum-drum echoes of a teacher–

"Tell me what follows a flat river?"
gradually picking up pace to become
more declarative– "What follows a flat
river?" Of course no answer, turning into
an explosion– "What follows a flat rivvva!"

Looking back on those days I realize how
resentful and repulsed and lack of respect
I had for these influences, those ruthless
disciplinarians and blathering idiots

(terror/bull teachers who take out their failures
on their students) yet somehow, obscurely,
from a sentimental point of view, miss too
this gruesome period of growth & development

the slim seductive girls with their long stares
and long hair; longing eyes, holy and hollow
with thick lips and thick accents, going
nowhere, looking to go anywhere but

there, somewhere…as though everyone
everything was so unfair and when you
get down to it very likely they probably
were…quite perceptive & keenly aware

not caring a lick about what follows some flat river
more so absorbed about their past than the future
or the forefathers of our great nation who
probably too would have taken advantage.

Treatment plan,

1. i think if those sectionals were around
   during freud's time he would lay out
   the whole goddamn fucked-up dys/funk
   chanel family unit and have them go at it
2. start chain-smoking those cubans
3. ingest a whole mess of coke solution
4. how do you translate "you could give
   a headache to an aspirin!" in austrian
5. outsource them to a skinnerian
6. start reflecting fondly again
   about those whining neurotic
   aristocratic jewish women
7. fire the interior decorator who
   came so highly recommended
8. "fucken schmendrick!"

I scream you scream (we all scream...)

It came by no mere coincidence how just the other day
I asked one of the boys I'd been seeing for counseling
if there was anyone or anything that was making him
feel at all sad or lonely and he simply looked up at me with
those great chestnut crestfallen eyes and innocently replied—
"I missed the ice cream truck the last three days in a row!"
and thought and thunk just a bit more and was going to
tell him that that wasn't what I was talking of but when
I thought just a bit longer and deeper and thought
you know if I had been running down the street
with my dollar waving in the breeze and the
ice cream man had taken off on me for like
three days in a row that would probably
make me feel pretty lousy and down
in the dumps as well and sincerely
did believe as though this image
might be the perfect metaphor
for all those disappointments
and multiple losses we suffer
from in our later existence
when we are supposedly
supposed to be all grown up
and complete and contented
when we try so hard for happiness
and always just seem to miss it
and at the end of the session
I wanted more assurance
and so to wrap things up
asked the same question

as he slowly naturally
picked his head up
without any hesitation
and responded– "You know, I told
you, about me missing the ice cream
truck for the last three days in a row…"

A fear of intimacy: one of those old depressed new england towns when industry leaves town,

Back then
you used to think
there were some girls
who were worth going
crazy for often of
a dirty-blonde
persuasion
up there
and down there
hair constantly
slicked-back
from the ocean
savoring summer
most of them
tomboys blushing
shuffling drifting
surviving dreary
days of YMCA's
gothic steeples
weathervanes
clocks & crosses
(where so much historic
and ancient spirit emanated
where the dandelions burgeon
at the foot of *misty-call* cathedrals
where a forgotten blue bell babbles
every so often hidden in the bleak belly
of a belfry clanging for clamoring klutzy
commuters stuck between Hell & Heaven)
when it was so humid
it might as well

just be
whiskey
& marijuana
& angel-hair pasta
bats patiently waiting
to perform their midnight
soliloquies, the crabapple trees
cradling some empty billiard room
long sweltering afternoons
where gay cowboy gigolo
got nothing left to do
but plant himself
in some parking lot
watching old women
getting hit by cars
He sports a cabaret
smile, subtle and suave
The sad sexless scholars
who still live with moms
wield wild windswept
handlebar mustaches
dungarees above ankle
bizarre & disheveled
engaged in Charlie
Chaplin shuffles
The lakeside girls of
pink dresses & sandals
whose fleeting sex appeal
welcome any lost sorry soul
who's up for the challenge
Loose ladies in stilts
looking to resolve
their trauma prosecuting pedophiles
trying to come to terms with impossible
fathers and real-life love lives of denial

An old timer camped out on the corner
like a petty thief trying to recapture
lost rhythms from childhood
Half-crazed traffic cop
half harmless
half hostile
showing off
karate chops
at the crosswalk
A throbbing truck
packed to the gills
with clowns 'bout to bust
The alcoholic painter
always flush-faced
winking at you
like a light-
house
in fog
It seems out here
all that's left are
old heroes & bums
& just you & your
lover with the desire
to pleasure each other
(in baths & windows
& cars & graveyards)
out of some kind of deep pain
and sorrow felt from a shared
and accidental type of trauma
while at the same time, negating
& mocking the absurd elements
of culture, naturally releasing all
societal burdens through sex
& soft silhouetted pillow talk
as familiar as some childhood

whisper, supper, foghorn
& trainwhistle– "Yeah, I saw
a paper falling off the bundle.
It was 3 o'clock in the morning
right there out there in Fall River."

Denouement of the dunce cap,

Reflecting back on the previous day
now wearing the mask of a therapist
feeling at times like a dummy or ventriloquist
really no different trying to make a difference
knowing it's probably the parents who are a
bunch of phony hypocrites having nothing at
all to do with issues behavioral or cognitive
(making such simplistic statements like
"manipulative," "attention-seeking" and
"at-risk") I visit my client or consumer
as some these days like to refer to it
in one of the library offices knowing
all he truly needs is a girlfriend or
someone who really gives a damn
about him and glance through the wavering
shadows of slanted blinds where I imagine
I can see the shimmering leaves of shady
sycamores transform right before my eyes
dancing against the ripe chilly belly of a
brilliant blue sky; the skyscraper pillars
which line cavernous insides of forgotten
forests that rise and climb with all their
might as though protecting a precious
piece of inner light. On days like these
you feel as though you can see the whole universe
tumbling and trembling, whispering and murmuring,
grieving and celebrating, living and dying, sighing,
evolving, radiantly imploding, rolling, receding into
the palpitating mountains and lungs of lost and lavish
lagoon trees, howling in a gushing gallery of red and
orange and yellow blaze leaves; in fact there's so much
you feel these kids are not revealing, restlessly stirring

somewhere between fantasy and reality; edification
vs education, if you can't get with the program go with
nature for everything of substance, everything that really
matters, lies in the lost romantic spirit of the resplendent
change of seasons, as here come the oil trucks and school
buses and fast-food girls over railroad tracks, the piano
men making their rounds beneath miraculous sugar
maples, the mad medical men behind haunted
shutters, holy crow who simply roams down
the road and makes his way from door to door.

Innocent until proven guilty or vice-versa
or whatever works best to their advantage,

Today I was at *The Dollar General*
      with my client
& there were these leftover
    chocolate crucifixes
from Easter & wondered
   what was the phenomenon
the point & purpose?
    Some good down-to-earth daughter
(a slice of heaven) taking
   itty-bitty bites or nibbles
while the raucous relatives
    with chemical dependency
problems get stupid
   off booze & moonshine & wine coolers
as wasn't Easter
    supposed to be about
his second coming
  or return or resurrection
& wonder
  if he ever imagined himself
on a chocolate cross
  in the dollar general store
right next to where
  that house burnt down in the center
of town
  across from the water treatment plant
& slaughterhouse.

Wonder if she had one of those
eating disorders
        or simply watching her figure
& left pieces
                of it in the freezer
next to the TV dinners?

Dysthymia,

While taking my lunch break strolling through *The Silver City
Galleria* I was feeling a mild case of melancholia and reflected
while hearing in the corridors murmurs of a song by Donna
Summer and thought that maybe perhaps I simply had not
come to terms with the disco era then heard the very next
day just outside *The Chocolateria* a kid had been stabbed
and murdered by some rival gang member as well as
in that selfsame quaint New England town someone
had broken into another resident's home and shot
the cat and defeathered the bird and thought maybe
really it had absolutely nothing at all to do with
disco or feeling an off shade of blue.

Pain diary,

Consider at the close
of some clinical day
when an array of stray
crickets show up at dusk
and long shadows caress
popsicle stick fences
some blessed breeze
and band of sunlight
wrapped around
trunks of trees
how you love
to ease back
in the patient's chair
how it feels so much
better in patient's chair
holding on for dear life
to some truth or dare
some hot tar roof
of a New England nightmare
a weathered hot-buttered wall
some clock that slowly revolves
Siamese sulking on top of table
wild wavering whispering of elms
room with its dysfunctional
and dismantled dollhouse
the bullshit and the brawls
the secret suicide scribble
the stories you never saw
the toy cars on splintered sill
the pastoral pictures on the wall
the hush of white noise in the hall
the peel of punch-drunk steeple bells

the sudden swell of ripe rivers somersaulting to Fall
that chair where you simply like to hang your head
there's something to be said about hanging head
sometimes all one can really do is hang head
to be wasted and full of a beggar's bread
more inclined towards wise man's dread
like everything else that lingers out there
the trees and shadows and Siamese
filthy and confused and redeemed
like rivers of fog spilling through
forests at the aperture of evening.

Dollhouse discovery,

When you know in real life
everything *is* in disarray
when everyone and
everything has strayed
all the roles and rules
rearranged (true-blue
symptoms of diss-
function loco-
motion
this house
is haunted!
family tree
which bends
and bleeds branches
and leaves of agony and pity
roots of grief and broken bark
of humility and active-enmity)
and the kids in pain
and parents drained
what's even worse
when it goes
the opposite way
and kids are dazed
and parents slain
when the father
gets deliberately placed
face-up in the armoire
like some dreamed-up grave
and mother and daughter
on the bottom floor
dismembered
body parts

scattered
shattered
looking
as grave
enslaved
left to waste away
in their stunned
and estranged
cell of shame.

Ritalin,

Kid did his
whole session
today in Count
Dracula fangs.

Father in jail,

The other kid showed up
with a machine gun and I
put my arms up and he took
me hostage all the way down
the hall as his mother smiled.
I asked him if he remembered
how to get to my office which
of course became something
of an adventure where we played
Operation and *Connect Four* as his
eyes magically lit up then sparkled
while somehow they diagnosed him
with an Adjustment Disorder and at
the end of the session he galloped back
down the hall with the spirit only a child
is capable of and think I even reminded him
of this and he took it all in stride and casually
nodded then I pondered "how else was he gonna
answer?" And returned him safely back to his mother
who took him out for a feast at *Chuck E. Cheese* or *Papa
Ginos* one of those family joints or another and we
scheduled a follow-up session to try and address
these "defiant behaviors" and thought to myself
perhaps maybe it's simply like how my lost mad
lover once put it that you can never tame a free
spirit then thought once more what could
I do to really help this child?

Sometimes it is of interest when you probe
their denial and ask them if they might recall
their first memories how they're so often
catastrophic and concrete then ask them
what they want to do when they grow up
suddenly turn vague with faraway gaze
or some lazy shrug of the shoulder.
You ever see a baby who just
couldn't seem to manage to
crack a smile on the subway?

Tourette's,

I used to have this friend
whose older brother had
Tourette's Disorder and
every Sunday evening
before the sun lowered
would climb with great vigor
to the tippy-top of poplars
in the back of his backyard
in the suburbs and holler
what we considered to be
some pretty hysterical and wild
lewd descriptive curse words
which went something like–
"You motherfucker! Go to hell!
Suck my…" In retrospect I think
we'd even feel a genuine sense
of remorse and pity maybe even
a bit of envy at the bold and brazen
heroic-like traits of his personality
that he had the balls to demonstratively
attempt to pull these things not really
understanding the severe nature to his
pathology. A matter of fact it turned out
to become something of a rather sobering
ritual and routine as eventually there was
no longer even a question every Sunday
evening when the firemen would arrive non-
chalantly with their long ladders and cherry
pickers to try and retrieve and plead while
he would scream at the top of his lungs–
"Go fuck…" Interestingly I believe there
was even that deep-seated anticipatory

feeling of anxiety somewhere around
late noon or early evening thinking
and knowing what soon might be
materializing and ultimately we'd
collectively feel a cathartic sense of relief
peculiarly and maybe even psychotically
developing and superimposing his own
trauma and grief empathetically onto our
own fragile beings acquiring the selfsame
maladaptive ways of dysfunctionally coping.

No one seemed to make very much of a stink
anyway as I think eventually we simply got
used to accepting it as something of an
everyday routine like the rooster crowing or dog
barking before the ominous evening would settle
the day before the week. I fondly recall the family
would even sometimes make this wonderful home-
made crumb cake or bundt with a cup of tea and
coffee that you deliciously smelled streaming from
the kitchen as though preparing for a future scene
knowing soon the night would be falling as you'd
see silhouettes of the firemen bringing him down
mechanically like a strange choir of fallen angels
descending from the trees when they'd all simply
be gathering in the family room conversing. I guess
ultimately this was the best way that he was able
to express his existential angst and pain and now
that I think about it just a little more I mean
a lot I really do miss those days…

Progress note,

Client informed clinician today
that he sleeps with those fangs to
replace bite plate the orthodontist
gave him. Clinician was curious about
role of mother and if she had had any
concerns about nightmares, night terrors.
It is also important to note that this was
the same mother when we provided family
stabilization services at domicile disclosed
while having a manic episode hx of domestic
violence and trauma while still wearing a hockey
mask and youngest child taking slapshots at her.
Family was originally brought to our attention
based on a charge that daughter had been fondled
by a foster child of next door neighbor and son's profound
feelings of guilt at not being there to protect her, mother's
poor coping mechanisms, confrontational behavior, and
possible Munchausen Syndrome, emotionally subjugat-
ing her son by constantly reminding him of that traumatic
episode, which apparently was a mask for her own symptoms
of possible drug use, Borderline, Bipolar…Clinician was
concerned about her lack of orientation, disassociative
presentation, and restless body language, which he felt
may not have only been symptomatic of a personality
d/o, yet might possibly point to a substance abuse problem.
The husband who was d.v. perpetrator and who had recently
been laid off simply sat in corner in a submissive manner
and clinician was able to feel a genuine amount of empathy
for everyone in home except for her. DSS was contacted
for precautionary measures and 51A was filed for possible
addiction to pain killers. Note too, that clinician felt close
connection to client picturing the image of him sleeping
with those fangs on.

Skyscraper graveyards,

The client I am working with after multiple years of neglect
down in the states of Florida and Texas who likens himself
to something of a chair or stop sign on the side of the road
finally got a good and thorough and competent diagnosis
because most of the branches at last died and fell off
his dysfunctional family tree, explaining in-depth
with great sincerity and earnestness in one of those
monotone tones his idea for skyscraper graveyards
and how it will conserve and save on the earth's
land and lawns and of course natural resources
where on each level and floor he would just roll
out swatches of astro-turf and thought as half-
crazed as that may very well sound really do
like the idea a lot and provided so much more
than clinical support and validation and even
told him it reminds me a little of a Dr. Seuss novel
like *The Lorax* simply only making the comparison
in sensibility and aesthetics of which of course with
the most literal and straightforward of responses and
explanations broke it down to how it would very much
be the opposite as we thus both drove with pensive
expressions I suppose thinking of those graveyard
skyscrapers rising majestically into the heavens
heading towards *Walmart* with his social security
check to pick up his chocolate covered cherries
for Valentine's Day of which he would keep
a very neat and organized account of
how many he ate on a weekly basis.

Asperger's,

Walking through
Walmart with him
I suddenly discovered
felt very much like traipsing
down the halls of a hospital
the psycho ward most
specifically but I guess
something of a respite
then heading back out
through the labyrinths
of the mall the different
color gumball machines
the little electronic hobby
horses to keep the 2-4
year olds busy and happy
as if zygotes rocking back
and forth in wishy-washy utero
the disoriented dope addict moms
the lumberjacks and mallwalkers
the teenage seductive blushing
girls I suppose the only consistent
whimsical entities of contemporary
society and civilization; the old timers
some of the few people I can relate to
then head back out to reality
to the parking lot all lined
by natural white birches and
felt like I hadn't been out there
for so damn long and having a bit
of a hard time grasping reality (which
felt strangely suspended and surreal
like some paint-by-number painting)

and took a great deep breath and looked
up to the sky before I crept back into
my car with my psychotic client
rambling with his racing thoughts
talking about everything possible
that didn't have to do with reality
as you look forward later on
maybe to a vodka & *Pepsi*.

The family stabilization team,

They used to always invite me after work to go to see the
young girls dancing. I don't know, even though I suppose
I may have felt honored, maybe even a bit flattered I always
felt that that just made me feel more lost and lonely. Anyway
those days were far behind me and had found I had a girl
back home who I loved and adored and found without a
doubt to be much younger, nicer and prettier. They were
good guys though from South Boston and Cranston, Rhode
Island and told them how much I appreciated the offer but
really looked forward to returning home to my new family;
had never really had much of one anyway and simply took
pleasure in returning home to her, as anyhow it was the end
of the day and strangely enough found her to be more
interesting. It was funny or guess might even call it
a bit ironic cause their wives were pregnant too and
were usually like the ones who were the head of
The Family Stabilization Team or even ran the
whole damn freakin' mental health agency.

Raised by dogs,

When I finally end up doing termination with that kid whose
parents raised him in a dog cage and time for me to leave
and move on, he just very politely inquires in the front seat
of my car if we can close our eyes and lower our heads and
say a quick prayer, and think am so moved and touched by
this, by all the obstacles and hardships he has had to endure
and think I could probably use a little of this myself, and sick
of all that obligatory and mandated social work bullshit
and semantics and code of ethics, while actually being
intimate and down to earth and human say of course
we can and just lower our heads in the dirty slushy
parking lot of winter outside the group home in
Providence. He's doing well and happy he is.

PART FOUR

STRAY DOGS, WINOS

TOMBOYS AND WHORES

Views from the meat market,

Gold-it dawn
    ambitious?

        he orders his steak bloody-raw
           dreaming through chilly windows

             with a view of the drag queens
       & hookers

             looking out over the cool blue
      cobblestone

     of the meat market
   somewhere below 14th

               in the mad streets
                  of Manhattan

       delinquents drifting home at dusk
   to their mothers' brownstones

(the suicide kids
& comedians

the stray dogs
& doormen)

     past play
    grounds

grayclouds
        past florists
              & old antique & cigar shops
                  morbidly-obese fortune teller
                      with fake nails

          devouring pork rinds
               turned off

         on a cell phone
           in neon

   of dim windows
& broken promises

         used musical instruments
     the immaculate pharmacist

           & knows he has great things
     in store for him

               what it is
        he knows not...

that he'll stray off course
but will never give up

   doesn't give a fuck
      what they say about him

     as deep-down inside
        sees this is as a sign of the weak
           and not very strong

even when they pull
the blinds down over the skyline

over bookshops
& barrooms

over bridges
& rivers

he'll still manage
to keep the vision

& make some-
thing out/of
him/self

even if his life depends on it
even if it kills him...

The angst of angels,

M Seeks F– to rub ice cube on chest in three-storey
walk-up. No experience required. Just a sensitive
touch and sympathetic outlook in the settling dust
of Summer's hustle & bustle maddening hypnotic
hush of sunset candles. All attitudes must be left
at the door. And we'll stand like shadows worshiping
the watertower in the mist then reveal our deepest
secrets in one of those ol' beat-up clawfoot tubs.

This will become our language or lack there of
while brooding gangs all return home down in
the dumps down cobblestone from a glistening
incandescent Ferris wheel of an out-of-town
Lower East Side traveling carnival back to
rag mop fire escapes of Chinatown after
all the madness and tragedy of humanity
chills out and calms down somewhere
between sundown and dawn.

Totally relieved, free and euphoric, we'll start our
relationship from the middle. Maybe even with a
squabble; listen to down-home blues from Chicago.

Dim room, flush of a fan
swaying Cleveland Pear
clang of church bells.

First breath on Pitt St. at dusk
disturbed tenants fall asleep
in darkened apartments.

I couldn't help thinking of my barber in The Lower East
Side with those deep wild Puerto Rican magical eyes, her
infectious laugh and convict brother in the picture frame
exclaiming– "What's up B?" – "Just chilling G!" then
lets out a hearty and healthy and haunted guffaw.

We had met under the bridge. She'd been nursing a bottle
of *Old Grand Dad*. It was raining. And when it finally cleared
and cleaned up the streets we made love on the rooftop
as I stripped off her nurse's dress revealing supple olive
breasts. She had a past and only fooled around
on the floor, as though she compulsively felt
the need to punish herself and had seen it all.

She used to be in a convent and had a blind father who
owned a string of bodegas in Yonkers. She was an alcoholic
and dragged around a bag with a forty and diary where she
was interpreting the bible in calligraphy. She said if she ever
got famous not to tell anybody about these things. I promised
her. And wondered why she felt the need to remind me.
Yet upon further introspection, I realized similarly, and
not too coincidentally, for many of the same, constantly
repeated reasons, was exactly the same way.

I lost touch with her just like everything else that Summer,
transient and fleeting (pals gunned down execution-style
and shotgun weddings, as though these celebrations and
tragedies were all a part of the same scene, remembering
graffiti banners swinging from scorching tenements, which
welcomed home older siblings from correctional facilities

like some strange slapstick comedy) historic and holy,
hypnotized by the heat while evaporating in an erotic

pool on Pitt St with hollering and screaming turning
to a muffled murmuring and trying to stay under as long
as I could, as long as all that doubt and damage turned
to relief and believing, celebrating my anonymity, yet
interestingly and ironically, increasingly feeling very
much for the first time a part of things. But I stray, I
stray, I finally stray. And somehow someway do believe...

There was no sound more soothing
than the birds warbling outside my window
when fog and mist spilled over the cathedral.

I pull a stocking over my head and
drink chocolate milk in the wind.

I turn away from anchormen because I don't trust them.

The super is beaten *with an* inch of his life.

Bob the Slob has a fish thrown
at him by the neighborhood kids.

And this is how it goes and this is how it is...

Before you go,

Tie up the fat lady & tickle her toes. Borrow a friend's
camera. Gargle in neon. Do impersonations while ambling
up the avenue. Wrap up sandwiches. Pawn TV in the snow.
Purchase a transistor. Pack two pints of brandy & if that's
not available *Mad Dog 20/20*. Unfold your ticket like origami.
Like a fortune cookie from New York City to Cleveland to
Chicago to Denver to Cheyenne to Omaha & San Francisco.
Admire lesbians speaking softly in the streetlight running
for their lives to the end of the night. Wave goodbye to The
Lower East Side. Mott. Hester. Ludlow & Orchard. To the
bridges & rivers & pawn shops & pianos. To dogs & neon.
Angels & hustlers. Throw rocks at wrong people's windows.
Embrace sirens. Flirt with nuns. Challenge tomboys to
thumb wars. Drink a cold one. Say a prayer to pigeons. Send
threatening postcards to old bosses. Sit down on park bench
& hear the tone-deaf orchestra. Have one final thought.
One final vision. Feel the breeze clear your throat. Dissect
shadows. Trace the shapes of women. Of Puerto Ricans
prancing like princesses to the sun. Girls in sandals shuffling
like angels. The last seductress smoking a cigarette on the
corner. Last child making cat-calls to the window. The last
pouting tomboy who chews out her boyfriend & the more
she does the more he gets turned on. Sport a smile impossible
for anyone to steal. One last drug deal between rich boy &
Rasta. Last old timer bringing home beer in the shadows.
The last desperate woman returning home without her
hero. The last pensive dog pondering like Plato. Unbutton
the bistro & finally get familiar. See the same liars repeat
the same patterns & be glad you're no longer a member
separating the accent from language. Make no decisions.

No promises. Forgive yet never forget. Turn inward. Have
no regrets. The last ditch dreamy tenement final curse word
that sounds sacred. Last child nursing her drunken father.
Shake off sorrow. Look crosstown not just to your destin-
ation but to where you once were & will one day return.
Ditch old habits & invent new proverbs.
Breakdown. Bitch. Brood. & blossom.

A reenactment of waking life,

Tuna & matzah & seagulls
        jerking off to young girls

           in their mid-twenties in pigtails
                playing softball

          with hand in pocket
              on park bench

      in schoolyard in The West Village
           that perv (who 'dat?)
                from *Archie & Veronica.*

Delinquents with mad heart
      scaling the center field fence
          & drag queen finally fighting back

kicking the shit
     out of some he-man
        alpha-male machoman

involving a broomstick
      flogging
        & very effeminate commands.

A bum gets picked up off the curb
     & declares– "top of the morning to you!"
          leaving them all in stitches.

You return home with chicken salad & seltzer
  & a new hardcover on that great author Thomas Wolfe
    & older southern belle you're living with

whose man just up & left her & now obsessive
                    & resentful & always telling you
                            to turn around when she's changing

            knowing exactly what she's doing
                        lifting up her tee & exposing
                                    those perfectly

        fragile tiny champagne glass titties
                    & you as always
                            (being 20 years her former)

        formally sneaking a peak
                    right into her *Pierre Deux*
                                faded dressing room mirror

                        & her having her daily dose
            of psychotic temper-tantrums
        full of loss & abandonment

threats & ultimatums–
        "I got knocked over
                by a deaf kid doing sign language!"

        You just want to dig into
                    your chicken salad sandwich
                            & *look homeward angel*

        as at such a young age
                    not quite understanding
                        her seductions & what I did to deserve this?

Denouement:

In retrospect maybe
she just caught you
sneaking a peek

into dressing room
mirror while she
wasn't looking

playing hard to get
& mad & upset
that you never

followed through
with all her feminine
fancy & folly & foul

glimpses of emptiness
maybe it was just
as simple as being

desperate & needing
some sort of young stud
to just get back at them all

& heal all the anguish
but more importantly
in one fell swoop

one final fuck
just to halt
& help

to somehow
finally try
to forget.

In retrospect
all kind of sick & ironic
cause when I finally moved out

would literally parade
by with her parasol
by my brownstone

right off
Bleeker
& 7th.

Those summers in the cobblestone of soho,

I remember this girl
I always tried to get
really close to was
impossible to get
close to and used
to visit me at the
bookstore and
was a cute girl
from Upstate
New York but
was like her
mood and
identity
changed
like sudden
gusts of wind
blowing down
cobblestone
and think
may have
even had
a case of
Borderline
or Bulimia
of which I was
totally sympathetic
and was like always
jumping in some cab
from my apartment
in Brooklyn at dusk
to try and save her
and barreling over

the bridge to Soho
like ghosts trying
to rediscover
to recover
all that had
been lost
back to
the true core
of self and being
and would ask me
these questions
to try and figure
me out or figure
herself out or
for that matter
figure us both
out like what
was my favorite
movie and that
perhaps maybe
being the anchor
for our empty reality
in those keen early
relationship scenes
and would really
think long and
hard about it
and come up
with some
by Bergman
and Bertolucci
and Fellini and
hers were like
"Home Alone"
and "Uncle Buck"

and could just
see her get
instantly
disappointed
(having no
idea how much
I already was…)
why I didn't like
or didn't get
or never saw
Home Alone
Uncle Buck.
I slept over
her loft
a couple
times just to
really try and
make things
work when
I was working
a late shift
at the book
store but
knew by
no fault
of my own
in my heart
of hearts
was only
fooling myself
one of those
unstable
relationships
just couldn't
get a hold of

constantly
dragging me
into maddening
scenarios and
as hard as I
tried just could
not make any
sense of
and futile
and would never
ever work out
(where they love
you one day like
you are their savior
and the next day
the cause to all
their problems)
and heard when
I took off from
the bookstore
she went back
a couple more
times to see
where I was
and in that
of course
she was
consistent
and always
around and
somewhere
to be found
after I was
long gone
and had

no choice
but to
move
on.

Radio (and falling asleep to an old coffee can of iced tea),

"And so The Mets down to their very last strike, one ball, two strikes." Don't know how bad that *really* is? Doesn't that remind you of some mad blissful sideyard garden creeping up childhood suburban bedroom window when the homegrown stalks of corn got larger than your young pretty hippie mom and you in your John-John overalls both standing there proudly with mutual smiles in a faded photo? The tiny sun-dappled pears glistening, lingering beneath bamboo curtains draped in the opened living room running into old girlfriends in the greenhouse in the rain? The ones who threatened you after you made love to them in the flashing Technicolor burning rooms of motels hidden away in Maine, while you offered them to live happily ever after with you in the trapdoor on the top floor of your castle in your tenement during Lower East Side days which stood like a wonderful dazed ashen black and white mausoleum looking down to The Manhattan Bridge still not completed after a decade, connecting nowhere to nothing and just wanting them to share with you in the eternal empty eternity, passive-aggressively getting back at you for all their abusive relationships with men, laughing and claiming they had AIDS, the whole hallway as always smelling like eggplant parmesan, rice and peas and sweet plantain, whole herds of gigantic trampling Chinese families and poor rich white girls getting involved in half-crazed relationships to try and once more believe and forget everything, getting ditched and winding up desperately lost and lonely, literal out-of-work clowns, wailing and howling

from their solitary midnight windows like shadowy portholes
overlooking the courtyard, and chucking vases at studs
returning home from the disco when they were off
their psychotropic medication– "and so The Mets
down to their last strike, one ball and two strikes…"

The charmed life,

Pondering
in Chinese
restaurant
parking lot
transfixed
in pitch dark
with streetlamp
on like that *Kojak*
where that dope addict
lies face up on a mattress
hypnotized by a lightbulb
bringing you all the way
back to early childhood
and a little bit later on

Exchanging warped faded vinyl record covers
of Jim Morrison and The Doors *LA Woman*
which blew you away and took you away
to a whole other place, ethereal, unimaginable
beyond the imagination, idealistic, spiritual
strip in Reno? Vegas? Palm Springs? L.A.?
A place you could never even fathom
liberated, vain, vulnerable, afraid
falling asleep to the whir of air-
conditioner, lost in the half-
awakened, semi-conscious
consciousness of sleepovers
in the hollow land of wasted
summer of suburbs, the only
scents you remember, leftover
smells of suntan lotion, burnt and bronzed
trying to keep that buzz going on in deep

dewy midnight grassy lawns which always
made you feel so lost and alone having
no idea where your life was gonna go

Always fascinated
by those guys
who spent
half their lives
in small towns
just hanging
around those
old time mai-tai
Chinese bamboo
half-moon Formica
fly-by-night bars
while you knew
no women would
ever walk inside
and pathetically
every so often
would feel the obligation
to glance up at the television
giving the illusion they were
busy doing something
or trying to convince
others that something
interesting was happening
some of them fishermen
some of them junkies
some of them gravediggers
some of them actuaries
some of them insurance salesmen
some of them compulsive gamblers
some of them still living with mothers

As the maître d' would lead young
and romantic eager lovers
and big bratty families
past fake Buddha's
and big fish bowls
to their tables

Who was that philosopher (*that rock-and-roll singer*)
who stated– "Most men lead lives of quiet desperation
and go to the grave with their song still in them?"

They said Springsteen's masterpiece was "Born To Run"
yet I derived so much more from and turned on by his
first one "Greetings From Asbury Park" and later on
"The River" which set my restless, romantic soul afire

Growing up in a rather overbearing
and dysfunctional Jewish family
I distinctly remember feeling instantly
connected akin with Dylan's– "Nobody feels
any pain/tonight as I stand inside the rain…"

It was the hippies who used to so fervently gather around
goom-bye-ya campfires, around The Beatles, "Sergeant
Pepper's" studying, deconstructing, playing it backwards,
claiming Paul had been murdered, yet so much more
preferred, and would have put "The White Album"
up against almost any other, and then shovel
it right down into the time capsule

Then it was The Who's "Quadrophenia"
the first group I actually ever remember
astutely, aesthetically combining the rumble
of the ocean with the rumble of rumbling teenagers
and self-soothing sound of old scratchy records– "I

don't mind other guys dancing with my girl" fading
off to the rumble of thunder– "Loo-ve! reign o'er me!!"

While just a little later on, a couple
years later, The Clash's, Joe Strummer
brilliantly fused and melded reggae and punk
in the working-class struggle turmoil of London

These were the only people I really trusted and could
spiritually and emotionally turn to during periods of crisis
when I felt half-crazed and the world was caving in and
coming to an end; the only ones who could possibly
understand, and would never ever let me down when
I felt down and out and there was not a soul around,
and just simply knowing I could turn on a simple song,
a simple sound, and instinctively, passionately, relate to
the beat and rhythm and murmur of a heartfelt soul…

Of some mentor-savior just as alone, who I also knew and
felt I could believe in, never betray me, providing a constant
genuine safe and secure sense of truth and belonging, even
helping to heal a bit the pain and suffering, remaining
indelibly etched in delicate imagination and transcendent
spirit of my consciousness at curfew; I used to literally fall
asleep with 2 or 3 carefully chosen records balanced on
the brink teetering on top my turntable, being held there
tightly, suspended in mid-air, patiently and politely waiting
then each one gradually, gracefully, slipping and sliding down
the pole with a slight and sweet subtle thud, like some classy
stripper removing her slipper submissively slithering to belly,
spinning, sending me off to a whole other world, whole other
being and reality, far more satisfying, then suddenly, what
seemed like some sort of self-motivated ritual and routine,
another single disk of vinyl would release, gingerly plunk
down, and fall to its knees as if it had its own personality;

the docile arm, like a thief in the evening, determined and
diligently, languidly lifting up, and needle gently touching
down to miraculously start playing; only thing it seemed
to me I had any real control over, provided any type of
consistency, true-blue feeling of reliability and loyalty, kind
of trying to remember, but not really, when it was I fell asleep
to what band and what singer, to what solo and what scene.

Days of air travel: a time gone by,

I don't know
don't it seem
our culture
our country
these days
simply
boils
down
to riding
on one
of those
big little
model air-
planes with
drippy messy
glue we made
as delinquents
sulking, scowling
from the windows
with a whole sarcastic
snickering crew of flight
attendants who don't give
a damn or give the impression
they don't even want to be there
moody, humorless, overwhelmed
and resentful, literally throwing
the food at you in the air
dazed and distant
as you respond
with feeling
down in the dumps
damned if you do

damned if you don't
dissed and deserted
put on the defensive
by the very offensive
like some abused kid
like what did I do
to deserve this?
Everyone short
with each other
disgusted
passive-
aggressive
without
a clue
charm
class or
manners
or a modicum
or baseline
of etiquette
I mean
where
the hell
did it
all go
wrong?
How did
this all
happen?
Don't
you
think
every-
one's

asking
the same
damned
question
or sadly
enough
not asking
this question
at all as we all feel
the gratuitous obligation
to clap aloud like the end
of some dumb daredevil
air show like some small-
minded mediocre audience
and crowd for some clichéd clown
or poor comedian when the pilot
or flight attendant throws out his
predictable punchline and makes
the announcement upon arrival
and give some faux gratuitous
pre-manufactured
round of applause
relieved and
contented
when
the plane
has landed
just to reach
our destination
without any
other sort
of drama or
confrontation

having lost
all interest
and imagination
conflicted confused
through model glue
dripping windows
as you don't really
give a damn about
the weather or views
remember when your
mom used to dress
you up in a suit?

The long-lost art of sportsmanship,

You know I remember
growing up watching
my friend's parents
playing tennis
seeming then
so much older
ancient arthritic
out of shape
slower reflexes
yet interestingly
paradoxically
appearing
to be moving
much faster
slapping
swinging
at the ball
in fast-forward
always with those
pathetic self-wrapped
adhesive bandages
or knee braces
sometimes getting
way too serious
and earnest
with wristbands
and headbands
as if this would
make a whole
hell of a lot of difference
as if overcompensating
for all things missing

falling to pieces trying
to keep up appearances
or some arrested stage
of development
some extension
of childhood and
adolescence yet
ironically always
very tough on
themselves
a matter
of fact really tough
beating themselves
up even bordering
on abusive cursing
calling themselves
names under their
breath sometimes
even looking up
to the sky for
some sort of
sign support
or guidance
as if searching
for some kind
of God or little
angel or long
lost relative
who would
help them
get the ball
over the net
and you now
know in retrospect
appears representative

of all those things
taken from us in
our existence
trying to get
some kind
of closure
or control over
while hollering
at themselves
things like–
"Come on Anne!"
"Damn it Bill!"
"What's wrong
with you Anne!"
(I think as a
kid I used
to even
snicker
a little bit
not sarcastic
or insensitive
but just didn't
quite get or
understand
why they
took it all
so seriously
and who they
were yelling at)
yet recently
when I stop
to think
about it
find I can
really relate

to all that
frustrating
futile
suffering
existential
angst and
you know
sort of wish
there were
more people
like this
these days
if you kind
of get what
I'm saying.

That real deep down feeling of desertion
and betrayal even worse than a girlfriend
breaking up with you,

You wonder what it's really like when you finally discover
Darth Vadar's your father? I mean it's gotta be a little earth-
shattering and damn difficult to deal with; to focus when
you gotta go in for your graveyard and check guests in and
out at the front desk of *The Trump International*; when you
take that train back and forth from Grand Central to the
suburbs with all those other aggressive asshole go-getters;
when you once more have to pay another visit to see your
behaviorist and with that brilliant soothing English accent
tells you not to give it too much significance and attention
and to try and live with the discomfort and move ahead with
your existence and you tell him all worked up and agitated–
"Doc! Did you not just hear what I said? My dad's Darth
Vadar! I don't know perhaps maybe I oughta see a
Freudian?" And head out with head hung low to catch
a breath of fresh air in the darkening dusk overlooking
the damp park as always just helps to provide a sense of
relief and calm while you simply look up at that nondescript
transcendent and nostalgic constantly flowing and flickering
tickertape as always helps you to belong and feel so much
more at home reminding you somehow that you are not
alone (and without even knowing it provides some sort of
form of desensitization) like the exact time and rain and fog
while there's something every so often to be said about
the sentimental and obvious before you dip down into
the subway and head back to your destination–
"Damn! Darth Vadar! Ain't that a mother?"

Your own personal version of a nightcap,

And so you're just standing on your back porch grilling away
happy as a clam, not exactly sure what the hell that means
with your wife having taken off at dusk for a little downtime
at the local library hearing the mother next door going
through her customary routine and ritual of hollering at
her monsters who told me she put them in Catholic School
cause both her and her husband had had really memorable
experiences, Jim Morrison crooning trailing off through
the screen window you forgot to turn off in your son's
bedroom… *The minister's daughter in love with a snake* while
you just stand there with your pitchfork full of marinade
in the air and for some strange reason satisfied and contented
in don't know how long and look up for the first time and
the first season losing yourself in the great big massive
deep dense oak just beginning to bend and blossom laden
with acorns then just like everything else in this perverse
puzzling and perfectly delicate universe just like the fireflies
and tree frogs just like the crickets and cicadas just like
the howling Catholic School mother just like Jim Morrison it all
dies down and start to think is it at all possible you might just
be starting to get it all now but know you're in a hell of a lot
of trouble once you start thinking that way and know too that
is an absolutely absurd notion and has to be false and there
could be nothing further from the truth cause there's really
no true or false to begin with in the first place (considering
the erratic and inconsistent behavioral patterns and poor
character of a chaotic human nature) or even for that matter
to fathom or imagine and from a Zen-Buddhist perspective
as well in this empty and hollow and unfair lonesome world
there's really absolutely nothing (never has been never will)
to get at all

The chicken tasted good though…

Human remains,

I.

I keep on forgetting nothing
I try to distance myself
(from my being)
& always return desperately.
I'm a man of many profiles
yet very few pleasures.
I am a romantic who craves
the solace of thrift shops
raggedy steeples &
the motels of America
(This is my domicile
my *damn asylum*)
I've been whipped by
seduction & claim o women
I want to meet the girl of 3 figures
(of shadow & profile & windchime sorrow)
& boy who spouts do-it-yourself miracles
with a vase of flowers for his language.
I can return to squalor & create beautiful porno.
I've been in 7 train wrecks & speak o languages.
I've given birth to 3 clowns & 5 delectable monsters.
I have a medicine chest which rests in the back of my
head with a cabinet that shuts by its own free will & volition.
I'm not positive if I'm exiting or entering the theater.
I've watched whole gladiator films
through the windows of barrooms
(like some erotic nightmare).
People keep on calling me funny
& don't know what they want from me.
I'm simply living this life

& dreaming of dying.
I see graveyards in countrysides
& in cemeteries beauty.
I have flirtation down to a science
more specifically, taxidermy.
I'm the greatest magician of them all
& have made whole audiences disappear
& when I was sure they were gone
taken several curtain calls.
I love watching fat women
having conversations
in foreign languages
(I want to strip them naked
& use their belly buttons
for springboards.
I want to dissect their whispers
& reserve a seat at their stoning
washing it all down with
lemonade & cookies).
I want to learn as little as possible
& discover great rhythms.
I have fallen in love with silhouettes
on bullet-ridden oceans.
I want to take a vow of violence
& beat someone out of their indifference.
I want to fill out a questionnaire
with simple true/false answers
deciding the fate of the free world
& watch it go up & curl & whirl
with the murmur & peel
of children's laughter.
I have discovered
what makes women
magical are their gestures
& this is the exact same behavior

that makes man filthy & repulsive
as the mysterious locomotive
rattles through culture...
Of thieves, hustlers, pickpockets & angels
immaculate criminals exchanging riddles
cavorting in corridors, cool & comical
while beneath leather, the vagabond
fingers her forbidden area, then
zippers & buttons & drops
knuckles into seashells.
I have finally arrived
nowhere without
hope or fear
& discovered
at last *I am there.*

II.

Let's make a day of it
to visit the spirits of ancestors
Beautiful blood-sucking teens
The Hasidim & drag queens
The bums of The Bowery
The deserted dolls of alleys
The Zucchini Bread Lady
The homebound doctor
who once made
house-calls
now bound-up
suddenly coming down
with a case of Social Phobia
The catatonic child on his rocking
horse rocking in winter window
The husband trying to get rid

of wife & daughters putting them
out on the lawn with fellow tchotchkes
The weathervanes & widow-watches
The bird on a wire eavesdropping
on extracurricular phone calls
The crosses & the crows
The coyotes & stray dogs
The piano tuner indisposed
in his self-imposed seclusion
The sleepwalking neighbors
on their tractors & mowers
The curmudgeon & ex-convict
& clockmaker & coal miner
The kleptomaniac mothers
who feel betrayed & cheated
The timekeeper & housekeepers
The psychotropic pill pushers
The exhibitionists & projectionists
The perverts & perfectionists
The empty aimless businessmen
drifting to stray sleazy peepholes
some time during lunch hour
in the prime of their life
prime-rib to go
The suicide girls
like tarnished pearls
who couldn't take it
no more now left to howl
down hellish e.c.t. halls
hollow dolls forced to
cleanse their souls
with highball shots
of chalky charcoal
having been discovered
trying to catapult their

bare naked bones
over barbed-wire
right into The East River
whose plaintive calls now
too closely resemble
professional mourners
The elevator repairmen
& panhandlers
The exterminators
& window washers
The filthy-mouthed tug boat captains
& phantom tow bridge operator
The dope addicts in boxcars
in trainyards under the stars
with their bibles & scars
& birds-eye peek-a-boo
views of shattered
shipwrecked skylines
The alcoholic painters
surviving off wine, suicide,
poor punchlines, prison,
lost widows & road kill
The dead end kids of dusk
of ghosts of gusts of
hushed whipping
wild wilderness
when there's no one
& nothing else to trust
The delinquents smoking
blunts trying to make little
to no sense of existence
by the railroad
by the river
by the foghorns
by the phantoms

The ice fishermen
fishing for old friends,
family and acquaintances
for clues, for redemption some-
where between Hell & Heaven
The cliff divers & contortionists
having entered a deep depression
feeling deserted & abandoned
when tourists leave them
in the sudden off-season
The old timer with transistor
stuck to each ear trying to
drown out despair listening
to staticy ballgames with a
queer and soulful stare, shirt off,
strands of silver hair, bronzed bald
head, wandering down boardwalk
settled & sure, as though involved
in some strange eternal dress rehearsal
for The Afterworld to meet his maker
the Lord, the sun & sand & ocean's roar
The willing widow still in her beehive hairdo,
paint-by-number clothes, jigsaw puzzle bones,
content making her rounds to a gigolo-husband
finally buried underground, washing it all down
with a bowl of borscht, bagels, blintzes, fish eyes
& chopped liver on black bread, Lower East Side
sunsets, Old Grand Dad & beer straight from the keg.

III.

You enter the land where the pines point backwards
Where the poison ivy people greet you with roses
Where rainbows blossom beneath bridges

Where the fenced-in jailers' wives seduce you
who just want to snuggle then sexual relations
as you'll take in all guilt & anger & reconstruct
kingdoms in the windy wilderness of steeples & prisons
behind time-stained curtains visited by fairies & phantoms
The crow obsessively parts his hair in your medicine cabinet
Sky-blue weather woman with grin predicts the apocalypse
A whole town controlled by teenage nymphomaniacs
who give fragile delinquents inferiority complexes
with lawnmowing husbands frothing at the mouth
Old ventriloquists with their teeth knocked-out
primped and laid-out and propped up in windows
Dummies in slippers wasted in front of television
Dead wives in disguise head of philanthropic
organizations who dish out looks of poison
based on their own
parasitic prisons and
can no longer rule
by axe of seduction
the dogs are all holy
Inhabitants, monsters
most interesting out here
are the really old women
who play electric mandolin
on the corner then siphon
the change out of their berets
for a little wine later returning
proud & contented back to their domiciles
all truth & emotion lies in the glistening
rain of cobblestone in the interlude in
the moment in the illusion of the episode
every one out here clean-
cut with nowhere to go
movie lets out & preacher scowls
bulletholes in the belfry

it's stripmall Heaven
wedding dresses in the windows of the railroad station
you can tell your future by all things not taught to you
something the cookie-cutter know-it-alls are still
desperately trying to convince (themselves) you
and look forward to natural disasters to write
haiku while willingly waiting a' top roofs
for the ice cream men & firemen
for the change of seasons
for a change of reason
chimneys back in action
thieves out to make a name for themselves
in an industrious no man's land of accusation.

IV.

Sister you saved me in my dream
after they shipped me away on the back
of some insane tow truck with all the madmen
& vagabonds, thieves & gypsies, the shirtless
gigolos & poor & pitiful lost souls, past the prisons
& mansions of false promises & betrayal, over the border
to paradise where they keep all the freaks they want to forget
about till eternity. You said you had heard all about the
accident from a witness who saw everything & with a
sweet & soft comforting voice said you understood &
showed me sympathy in some strange opaque foreign land
along the sea. When I stumbled off in my loin cloth to the
broken down resorts you could see that I was dazed & half-
crazed, disoriented & lost & with head dropped nothing
need be said & knew somehow you'd never forget.

Sweet millie from the borough of brooklyn,

With water tumbling down
I collapse in the shower
like Brando intoxicated
Jack the Ripper
Van Gogh
maybe even a young
Paul Newman in his
clawfoot tub in the
back of the carousel
in gangster Chicago
and think of sweet Millie how
I hugged her buck-naked shivering
solitary and secretive in the shower
in the bleak morning at the industrial
midtown Manhattan hospital overlooking
The East River with all the foreign and
familiar huff and puff tugs and barges
when all the down-in-the-dump buildings
were just getting up silhouetted in the holy
fog and smog of ole time New York and
all the know-it-all nurses, psychiatrists and
interns didn't have a clue and got one over
on them breaking every regulation and rule
but didn't give a fuck 'cause was desperate
and needed her and she needed me (this was
our therapy and in retrospect the best therapy
and only thing which held meaning as without
us even knowing, rebelling against all forms
of present and previous absurd oppressive
'institutionalized' authority, asserting our
independence and individuality and within
that one single glazed, dazed, bleary-eyed

moment becoming complete) sneaking
in there and hooking-up, hugging and
soaping each other up before every-
one got up; my excited cock rubbing up
against the smooth olive skin of her butt
before the day's daily routines and rituals
of mandated monkey milieu therapy
beautiful stunning Puerto Rican
Mami who was in her early-thirties
taking care of her boy in a brownstone
out on Bushwick Avenue, Brooklyn
and all the other patients returning
dazed and disheveled like zombies
in bathrobes to supposedly heal
deal with do or die depression
a shock of frazzled hair looking
like they had smoke coming out
of their ears having been given
the ultimatum against their own
will and volition of electric shock
treatment or a visit and extended
stay behind shadowy foreboding
gray bars of Bellevue being scraped
off the fence trying to make a mad
dash for it to the manic rapid racing
East River blood-curdling zombie-like
primitive anguished plaintive howls as
if just coming out of it and suddenly
realizing it all being escorted down
distant damaged far from home
tragic halls feeling she let down
everyone and worst of all herself
like some self-conscious self-loathing
fragile shell single solitary funeral
procession after being deserted

and abandoned by Lower
East Side boyfriend
young pretty Irish
girl trying it once
again from The
Hell's Kitchen
section of
Manhattan
adopted feeling
unwanted void and
vacant seeing way too
much of her brothers
in the Irish Mob
maim and murder
and take out
competitors
and all coming
back to haunt her
the guilt and torture
having to drink down
charcoal concoction
so she was there
for safety and
myself sorrow
seeing way too
much of the world
at way too young
of an age my best
friend jigged to death
small intestines hanging out
laughing afraid on sidewalk
pal shot down execution
style and trying to hold
brain together hysterical
picked up hitch hiking

trying to be molested
and taken advantage
by pedophilic
homosexual
yet eventually
we had to leave
and face the world
again as it all comes
back a little later on
somewhere between
the near and remote
future as soulful and
sentimental solitary triggers
when taking midnight baths
in Lower East Side apartment
with a sweltering summer window
open looking out to all of beatdown
lower Manhattan like some liberating
revelation like our version of freedom
and switchblade bridges which crossed over
to Brooklyn with wildly-lit flashing carousel
from the traveling carnival when all those
Chinese gangs returned home homeless
brooding beaten and defeated
heads bowed with girlfriends
feeling just as lost and cheated
and imagine Tony Perkins
and his sudden surprise visit
and kick the crap out of him
and meet Maria in the schoolyard
and we light out to East Orange
on some bus from Port Authority
in some deep muddy brown
second-hand passed-down
suit passed-out from nodding

out on heroin as we all apparently
need a place to escape to at times
behind shower curtain of old time
black & white silverscreen stars
staring into the drunken
bleary eyes of W.C. Fields
up the skirt of Marilyn Monroe
scrub the back of my earlobes
run my fingers through my hair
over cheekbones and hard-on
I'm not ashamed to think of her
of her tiny tits and trembling fears
then releasing tears between real
sweet red pussy hair alabaster
milky soaking thighs said she
got turned on by my small talk
watching juices semen vaginal
discharge flowing like all the
world all the cobblestone
after massive storm
letting it all go
wondering why should I go
I could stay in here for days
and no one would know
like John & Yoko
only I'd be
in the shower
getting reborn
I'd have revelations
but it's a cold-water
flat and gotta get up
past Hepburn and Chan
best vacation I ever had
imagining it was childhood
without walls or obstructions

and suddenly hear the cops
rapping at my door only I'm
wrong the blockbuster show
Real Stories of the Highway Patrol
throwing a black man to his belly–
"You have the right to remain silent"
one of the only true rights afforded
the broke black man in America
and think damn right the right
to remain silent you're telling
me after just contemplating
coming out of the tub
The right to remain!
The right to remain!
The right to remain?
All's any of us trying
is to find some place
to remain some hiding
place some secret hideaway
some safe & secure sanctuary
to once more finally catch up
and reunite with our sanity
to "serve and protect" our
self-respect and dignity.

I always liked the john adams,

I always liked the john adams…
i liked the fact that my older sister
had an apartment in the john adams
i liked the fact that the john adams
was an all white brick building
i liked the fact that it was supposed to have a doorman
and i never saw him and he was never at his station
i liked the fact that it was on 12th st and 6th avenue
i liked the fact that they didn't put a 13th floor on it
'cause back then they were superstitious and none
of the buildings around those parts had a 13th floor
i liked the fact that it was lined in lonely linoleum
literally surviving a whole summer off milk
and seltzer and gizzard and fried chicken
i liked the fact that it had a tiny little terrace
and swear read all of "finnegan's wake"
and "ulysses" just didn't understand
the gaelic or shakespeare references
so turned to kerouac's "subteranneans"
which helped to cure my insomnia
i liked the fact that i could hear
the constant wild and mad throng
of faraway cop cars and fire engines
holy and histrionic doing their emergency
rounds which always seemed to ground me
and strangely, perversely, brought me closer to humanity
somewhere between hell and heaven no longer abandoned
done-in and able to make a real downhome connection
i liked the fact that i had an on and off relationship
and ghostly rapport with the late-night soft whooshing
elevator doors in the hall which welcomed all freaks
and foreigners just as lost and lonesome as myself

i liked the fact that it had one of those self-soothing
air-conditioners in the window keeping me cool
during the brutal sweltering season of manhattan
i liked the fact that i could jerk off in silence
i liked the fact that it had that odd and peculiar
after-hours cable for those bachelors not getting
any; the strange sex channels and midget wrestling
i liked the fact that it felt like an all too sane single's sanctuary
for those half-crazed aristocratic daughters in publishing
or advertising or turning to high finance or lowering
their standards and marrying their psychiatrists
(having had it after the blind date circuit left them
dazed and distant with meltdowns, psychotic episodes
and suicide ideations doing respites being transferred to
bellevue "when they're fed up and can't take it anymore")
i liked the fact that there were absolutely no facts at all
when avenues and those long transcendent wanderings
in starving soulful streets and sawdust meat market
on the river would meet always ending up smelling
and stirring into one delicious aroma when you
were at the end of your rope which provided
an instant panacea to deliver and awaken
the senses in the wild warmth and stray
scents of cobblestone and chicken bones
and bums having given up on the world
and you feeling just as lost and alone
measuring your mortality between
that moment in time when you felt
eternally stranded and so damn
deserted with absolutely no one
to turn to somewhere between
the asphalt in the park and the solitary
stars still somehow stark-alive breathing beating
blaring through some silhouetted swathe of smog
i liked that fact that i didn't care (matter of fact

looked forward to it) from stifling heat impossible to escape
the steamy streets if i passed-out right there on the spot
getting all woozy and dizzy and blacked-out and
if i did drop dead god bless would finally die
a happy man right there on bleeker & 7th
and just drop me off right where they
drop off the morning papers right
below the glowing streetlamps
where all the hustlers from
the neighborhood the winos
and prostitutes were taking
whore baths below the cascading
flow of fire hydrants with soap
and shampoo making jokes
and cracking-up as if the first
and last day of the world as if
all reborn all within the moment
i liked the fact that i felt like kafka
still not sure of what i was being
accused of alienated at a loss and alone
and the john adams always made me feel right at home
i liked the fact that it was chock-full of artists and dope
addicts and geriatrics and college students which at
the time felt like most of the population of manhattan
i liked the fact that it always fell in between different
phases of my existence, life-transitions, thus putting
it all in perspective, having revelations, and trying
to make it last as long as i can, like someone
who does not take their freedom for granted
i liked the fact that it felt like the core nucleus
to the empty vacant radiant glowing soul
like some porthole to all things palpable
you did not care to be nor wish to know
i liked the fact that it always felt like some sort
of beacon or a place where you could stagger home

when you were really in need of a place to stagger home
i liked the fact that you could smoke blunts and drink bottles
of *merlot* from that liquor store on the corner and finish it all
off with leftover tortellini chilling in the refrigerator
i liked the fact (this one not so much) that i used to
wake up to her cat plopping right on top of my head
and so upset picking him up and flinging him across
the bed for some buffoonish brutish reason repeating
this routine and ritual over and over and over again
and for that i feel slightly sad and this is an apology
letter to both you randi-jo and your cat spencer
i liked the fact that it felt like the land of one-night
stands but was always a diehard romantic and
perhaps just overcompensation for something
at the time that i knew i just could not have
i liked the fact that it helped to escape "the act"
and seemed to survive a whole summer off
one pull-out sofa one towel one suicide
note love letter and one long-lost howl
i liked the fact that me and my pals
(i guess what the know-it-alls would
call oppositional-defiant and acting-out)
used to toss eggs at young couples talking
corny to each other during candlelit suppers
in courtyards way down below and then
all of a sudden look up bewildered
trying to find out where it came from
i liked the fact that the john adams
just felt like some blissful spiritual
hangover and even though i know
nothing really did felt like something
liberating and magical had happened
having all burdens lifted the night before
i liked the fact that it had a killer view of all
of lower manhattan (the secret rooftops of drag

queens and scholars and single women on suicide
watch and mothers and madmen abandoned all seeming
passed down from generation to generation somewhere
between clotheslines and watertowers) the confluence
of the east and hudson rivers and world trade center
and the lady in harbor feeling it all subliminally spiritually
stream together like when the lower east side immigrants
in rags to riches black & white schmatas came tumbling
in on a mission through fog & mists to make something...
i liked the fact that i liked the fact that i liked the john adams
which stands like some keen memory of a loyal and lifelong
companion, rock-solid, reliable, and responsible, eternally
etched in my desperate and fragile consciousness forever.

The natural formation & configuration of perimeters & boundaries: somewhere between the dunes & bones of old motels & liquor stores,

Abstract: Wow out here there are whole towns
just of motels & cottages of lobster & liquor
of burnt-out drive-ins making resurrections
real weary wanderers of no direction
& no place I feel more comfortable

Proof: Upon driving out here casually present to my wife
a whole new psychological concept and theory of mine
where I sincerely think and believe an individual in self-
imposed isolation for one reason or another or sincerely
because of specific circumstances or stressors and anxiety
can get so excruciatingly lonely literally develop the exact
selfsame psychotic symptoms and traits and characteristics
(which may overlap and parrot) and even materialize
(even if not organic) into a whole other pathology of
let's say a severe diagnoses or disorder such as schizophrenia
and provided here for example that psychological phenomena
of a boyfriend and girlfriend always constantly around each
other as he happens to have one of these profound disorders
while she literally can develop or pick up the exact same
symptoms or inability to function or maladaptive thinking
or bizarre behavior from this cultural and psychosocial
environment as if exacerbating and triggering and
creating a whole new different predisposition

Point being think people can get so damn sad (and lost)
and lonely may actually trigger whole other similar-like
symptoms and give the impression of other pathologies
which previously in the past may have only been isolated
or targeted to some other specific psychological disorder
without either having the chemical imbalance in the brain
or clinical criteria opening the door and crossing over
to some other unknown form which once lay dormant
but now stirring and active in the category of something
prodromal crippling and breaking down already rather
fragile and vulnerable defense-mechanisms and manifesting
 itself into something quite profound and intense and relevant

Clinical Conclusion: Wow out here whole towns
just of motels & cottages of lobster & liquor
of burnt-out drive-ins making resurrections
real weary wanderers of no direction
& no place I feel more comfortable.

Phenomenon's: swimming back to the safe (and secure) shores of alcatraz,

1.

I don't know how much I necessarily believe
people for all intents and purposes, or even
by nature, are self-destructive, but think it's
something far deeper and shallow, based on
a consistent psychological history of a constant
barrage on the senses (which cause them eventually
to decay and waste away, get withered and fragile)
and inundating of an overwhelming (and overbearing)
amount of emotional and spiritual abuse and damage
with tormenting patterns which get repeated
over and over (similar to those for example
who experience a similar amount of trauma
and feel in constant conflict, cheated, taken
advantage, or pervasive feeling of low-lying
depression, clinically-stated, of *dysthymia*
which plays itself out in self-loathing
and have no choice but to act-out or
to fulfill that "self-fulfilling prophecy"
in order just to assert their identity)

2.

These self-destructive patterns and tendencies
may even become something hardwired
characterologically or behaviorally,
a certain sort of acting-out on the
self (when the fragile ego and identity

has been so inundated and profoundly
stripped and torn-apart, and eventually
literally feel "got no choice" but to take
it out on themselves) caught in the literal
Hamlet Dilemma (stagnant, brooding,
pensive) caught in the "fight or flee"
psychological phenomena and turn
inwards towards isolating and self-
deprivation (for necessary instinctive
primal purposes and needs of coping
and survival mechanisms) which can
only eventually, realistically, in the long-run,
emotionally and psychologically, take them
so far until all got left is "self-destructive"

3.

For those who have suffered years of emotional
and spiritual abuse and neglect (tormented by
sleazy manipulation and treated like a possession
having their identity and ego stripped from them)
it comes clearly as no surprise and something of
a perverse psychological phenomena as well
as lifelong reality to feel like they're always
on-the-run (watching their backs in a state
of constant paranoia and on the defensive)
while strangely enough paradoxically like
wanting to swim back to the shores
of Alcatraz in the hopes to feel
(a part of and redeem and
restore) and feel more
safe and secure

4.

The metaphor for those abuse victims
who always whether aware of it or not
go back to those similar and selfsame
abusive situations swimming back to
shore and prison out of a self-loathing
and a self-fulfilling prophecy (as if they
deserve it and don't know any different
even putting on themselves strict boundaries
of a constructed self-denial and asceticism)
in the idealized hopes and wish to try
and be rescued able to connect with
the confines and containment of that
existence (and the core configuration
of that experience which has now been
hollowed-out in their long-term psyche
and consciousness) and other like-minded
prisoners (able to relate to) who may
too have had similar-like experiences

5.

How these prodromal symptoms
and traits and characteristics
become like the existential
stage and phase of escapism
and of course circle backwards
and forwards (dys)functioning
in the other direction vice-versa.

Planet Zero: i'll send you
a rose and then kill myself,

Before:

Picture the image of poor
polar bear just sitting there
stranded on that broken off
slab of glacier sailing helplessly
out to sea seeing smoke rings
meaning absolutely nothing

this time
the revolution
will be televised
not sponsored by

coca-cola, mydol
or jesus christ...

who sang that song again?

"i feel the earth move
under my feet, i see
the sky tumbling down
a tumbling down..."

In Between:

Her kiss seemed like the petals
falling off a rose the last stop
on the soul train when you
had nowhere else to go...

In the final end and existential apocalypse it will just
be two caucasian tourists pointing their smart
phones right at each other the prey and
the predator the captor and the captured
pretty much interchangeable with
their literal clinical delusions
of grandeur believing they
are the perfect witnesses
and reporters who have
caught each other and
shoot their built-in
cameras back & forth
forth & back
at each other
(focus/fixated)
till the end of time and
eternity, mistaken identities
mistaking identity (delusionally
believing they're capturing
some meaningful moment
paradoxically catching
themselves in this shell
of a futile obsessive-
compulsive routine
& ritual showdown
victims to
their own poor
miserable
moral fiber
aloofness
cookie-cutter behavior
and playing possum)
will bring it back like

some hero or martyr
to their psychosocial
environment
as if doing something
special for the rest of
reality show existence
theater of the absurd
nothingness having
gone back and forth
the ultimate exclusive
satirical idiots
of ridiculousness
completely unaware
of it and all that's left
is one stripmall
with one *7-11*
in the midst
of some vast
vacant wisp
of desert
still with
fresh lottery
tickets and those
milkshakes
you can
bake in the
microwave
at your own
convenience
to help to
heal the
blues and
doldrums
and emptiness
of existence

screen overhead
constantly repeating
over and over
and over again–

"how to approach
your doctor about
binge-eating disorder
tips to start the conversation…"

How to decorate a psychiatrist's office,

I.

Consider black & white pastoral prints
perhaps even cutouts or etchings

of some anonymous countryside
somewhere on some hillside

maybe in turn of the century
Russia, England, or Ireland

as you ascend a rear
set of stairs somewhere

in the switchblade dusk
of brilliant blaze leaves

and opaque pastel
horizons of Autumn

then leave without symptoms
some time around sundown

casually drifting home
(*dreaming of Whitman...*)

some place around The Long Island Sound
where nightmares end and dreams begin.

II.

The only shingle you'll hang
will simply say– "Eggs"

for when orange-blossom sun
comes and cranes fly away.

III.

Consider something between
a flesh-tone and bone

A gray or ghost
earth or wind-blown

Shadow and stone
dusk and dawn.

Somewhere between reality and fantasy lies the season
of your penetrating, palpitating, solitary soul, home…

IV.

When black crow
turns purple

and seagull
shade of blue

disappears to
the setting sun.

V.

[*Psychiatric Notes*...dx: Highly-intelligent
yet might present as simply good con-artist

His answer when put forth the question–
"How do you feel about family and friends?"

That they always appeared
hostile and jealous, threatened

as evidenced by their body
language and expressions

Could con or charm anyone.
Ma always said my tongue

would one day get me into
a whole hell of a lot of trouble

yet in fact got me in and out of
a lot of doors, seeing the world

(The stray dogs at the end
of the world on cold winter

boardwalks of Coney Island
and Red Hook, Brooklyn

who first tried to frighten
and then fed them chicken

and looked out together in silent snowfall
of dawn to the Statue of Liberty with just

the sound of chiming cowbells
then later on looked out for me)

and wouldn't trade that
for all the tea in China.

Claims to sincerely be intrigued
by how accents came to be

hypothesizing topographies, lay of the land,
patterns of weather, structures of cities…

By borders, straits of water,
when signs at train stations

naturally, gradually started changing
their language and letters, separating

very cultured, sophisticated
and mythological societies

feeling his whole life cheated,
filthy and empty, challenging

every (go) figure authority
just to make a name…

Short-term and long-term goals for treatment:
To restore client's self-respect, self-esteem, dignity

VI.

Peek through cactus
of half-bathroom

and close eyes
and imbibe

pure smoky breeze
cedar-burning chimneys

VII.

As one day you'll look to suddenly
secretly collapse in your study

of blush
of coral

like the sun naturally falling
like some stray pile of leaves

while your wife discovers you
and simply goes for the rake

raking you up
dumping bones

final expressions
words and all

in the wheelbarrow
carting you off

where you may finally rest in peace
eternally smelling biscuits & gravy

with a whole mess of wild stray
seagulls squawking above me.

Power of the poppy,

I would have loved to have been
one of Freud's persnickety patients

simply lying there stretched-out
somewhere on the outskirts

deeply immersed
in a hypnotic trance

under the influence
of the cadence

of the rhythm of one of those bucktooth
beautiful Black Forest coo-coo clocks

with maybe the window
cracked open just enough

to hear the blast of bluebirds
and smell the sweet fragrance

of a pungent perennial garden
with symptoms of persistent

persecutorial and conspiratorial
delusions not so much psychotic

but more so reality-based acquired
from all the overwhelming horrible

patterns of the gossip and rumors of
vultures of culture, of human nature

(You'll even offer hypotheses
of 'Survival of the Sleaziest')

A little high with a buzz
on off one of his famous

Cocaine-Dope-Manischewitz solutions
to help ease some of the tension

and pain and suffering of existence
hoping to shed some light into the

addict of a heartbroken brainwashed
manic-neurotic-romantic to try and

recapture that one single glimpse-moment, surreal dream
fantasy from blissful innocent ephemeral elusive childhood

and make sense of all that passive-aggressive
flirtation, innuendos & interludes (exhibitionism)

from seductive school teachers
oversexed grammar school kids

pleasantly confused either by hoof beats of horses
or practical pumps of working girls in the far-off distance

departing at dusk overtaken by cicadas and crickets…
Symphony of tree frogs and Magritte's illusory sunsets

sensing the cruel violence in the not too distant future
neither by chance nor coincidence but more so intuition

Man's rotten core based on self-interest
and his 'will to power'…to be malicious

swinging my feet off his love seat feeling a mild
sense of liberation from all pressures and happen

to mention how you might want to move to Maryland
as you've heard so many lovely things about its shores

more specifically, Casey Stengel and *The Baltimore Gold*
and passionately stroll home in hand-me-down coat

You'll turn on talk radio
when you get home…

Acknowledgments

Thanks to the following in which some of the poems in this collection previously appeared, sometimes in different form.

Paradigm Magazine
Hospital Drive: The Literature And Humanities
Journal Of The UVA School Of Medicine
Contemporary American Voices
Thought Notebook Journal
Panic! Brixton Poetry
Spirits: Indiana University Northwest
Weird Cookies
Curbside Splendor
Carcinogenic Poetry
Boston Poetry Magazine
Right Hand Pointing
In Other Words: Merida
Out Of Our
Poet Works
Stanley The Whale
Two Thirds North
42 Magazine
Centrifuge
Smoky Blue Literary and Arts Magazine
Ray's Road Review
The Vein
Crab Fat Magazine
Quail Bell Magazine
Epigraph Magazine
Transcendent Zero Press
The Sunflower Collective
Bluepepper Literary Journal

About the Author

Joseph D. Reich is a social worker and displaced New Yorker who really does miss dis-place and lives and works out in the state of Vermont. He has a handsome little son with a nice mop of dirty-blonde hair, and a wife eleven years his junior who must have the patience of a saint, as raising two boys. Being displaced and from New York, he misses most of all Shanghai Joe's in Chinatown, all those wonderful Russian and Polish diners of the Lower East Side, used to spend days on end haunting, and Dominick's in Little Italy, the Little Italy uptown on Arthur Avenue in The Bronx. He hopes one day to return to these places to play and pray and contemplate with his wife and kid in all those brilliant, scenic parks—most of all along the river on the Westside Highway.

Reich has been published widely in an eclectic mix of print and online literary journals both here and abroad, and has been nominated five times for the Pushcart Prize. His many books include *The Derivation of Cowboys and Indians*, *The Housing Market: a comfortable place to jump off the end of the world*, *The Hole That Runs Through Utopia*, *The Defense Mechanisms: your survival guide to the fragile mind* (Fomite Press), *A Different Sort Of Distance* (Skive Magazine Press), *If I Told You To Jump Off The Brooklyn Bridge* (Flutter Press), *Pain Diary: Working Methadone & The Life & Times Of The Man Sawed In Half* (Brick Road Poetry Press), and *Drugstore Sushi* (Thunderclap Press).